Caring for Your
Cherished Objects

THE WINTERTHUR GUIDE

EDITED BY

JOY GARDINER AND

JOAN IRVING

Winterthur Museum, Garden & Library
5105 Kennett Pike
Winterthur, DE 19735
winterthur.org

Distributed by
Rowman & Littlefield
4501 Forbes Blvd., Suite 200
Lanham, MD 20706
rowman.com

Caring for Your Cherished Objects: The Winterthur Guide was generously supported by Furthermore: a program of the J. M. Kaplan Fund

Furthermore:
a program of the J.M. Kaplan Fund

Copy edited by Onie Rollins & Teresa Vivolo

Designed by Barb Barnett, barb barnett graphic design llc

Printed in the United States through Porter Print Group, Potomac, MD

Library of Congress Cataloging-in-Publication Data

Names: Henry Francis du Pont Winterthur Museum, author. | Gardiner, Joy, 1955- editor. | Irving, Joan, 1959- editor. | Landrey, Gregory J., writer of foreword.
Title: Caring for your cherished objects : the Winterthur guide / edited by Joy Gardiner and Joan Irving.
Description: Winterthur, DE : Winterthur Museum, Garden & Library, [2021] | Includes bibliographical references.
Identifiers: LCCN 2020051736 | ISBN 9781538142516 (paperback)
Subjects: LCSH: Heirlooms--Conservation and restoration.
Classification: LCC NK1127.5 .H46 2021 | DDC 745.1028/8--dc23
LC record available at https://lccn.loc.gov/2020051736

Contents

Foreword

I have had the pleasure of being involved in the conservation profession for more than forty years, first at a cabinetmaker's shop connected to an antique store and then at Winterthur Museum, Garden & Library. It is true that conservators and scientists do amazing things in assessing and conserving objects of personal, historic, or artistic interest as images in this publication will show. However, it is you, the caretaker, the one holding this guide and reading these words, that can do the even more impressive work of preserving, stewarding, and giving meaning to treasured objects. Take the time now to familiarize yourselves with both the mindset and techniques presented here and be sure to explore the many resources identified by the contributors. You, your collections, and generations yet to come will all be beneficiaries of giving heed to the good counsel you will find in each page of the *Caring for Your Cherished Objects: The Winterthur Guide.*

GREGORY J. LANDREY

The Dwight and Lorri Lanmon Director of Academic Affairs
Winterthur Museum, Garden & Library

Introduction

JOY GARDINER

Cherished objects and family heirlooms hold a special place in our lives. Whether they are personal letters, grandmother's silverware, or the favorite stuffed animal from your childhood, these items all have significance and are part of your cultural heritage. As members of the preservation / conservation community, we applaud your efforts to care for these objects properly.

Seeking reliable information about how to prolong the life of the items in your care is certainly worth the effort, but today it is all too easy to rely on suggestions found through the Internet. A recent search for "how to clean antique silver" quickly yielded thousands of results. But how reliable is that information? Will it help or harm the things you hold dear?

The authors whose work is found in this volume all have extensive training and expertise in their area of specialty and a passion for their topic. In addition to overseeing the collection at Winterthur Museum, Garden & Library, we teach, consult, and lecture on the care of cultural heritage to graduate students, professionals, and the public. The experience that comes from answering questions over many years gives us exceptional insight into the types of information that can be applied to understanding the care of the special objects in our lives.

One hears the terms *preservation*, *conservation*, and *restoration* when discussing objects of some historical, artistic, or personal value. These terms overlap somewhat but cover different portions of the care spectrum. **Preservation** is concerned with keeping damage from occurring and with slowing down the degradation processes. It is the main goal of "preventive conservation," which is addressed in the opening chapter. **Conservation** builds upon this goal and may also include the active treatment of objects. A conservation approach includes understanding the materials used to create the object as well as documenting the current state, the known history of the object, and the structural and/ or aesthetic treatment. **Restoration** involves returning an object to an original or previous state, which may necessitate removing more material from the object than in a conservation approach.

The purpose of this book is to provide practical information so that you can care for your objects in an informed manner. The first line of defense is always preventive conservation. Knowing what you should and shouldn't do is crucial. Knowledge of materials is also of paramount importance in helping you understand how objects change over time and what the susceptibilities to damage might be. Finally, advice about proper storage and display will aid in providing an environment that is conducive to prolonging the life of your objects.

Science is an integral component of conservation, and Winterthur is fortunate to have a well-equipped Scientific Research and Analysis Laboratory. Our scientists, Rosie Grayburn and Catherine Matsen, have written sidebars for each chapter that address the application of science to the understanding of cultural heritage objects and their care. Also included are the procedures that can be safely done by an owner as well as those that require the services of conservation professionals.

With the knowledge gained from this publication, you will be better able to assess your possessions, understand which objects are most vulnerable, and avoid the situations that will put them at more risk.

CHAPTER 1

Preventive Conservation

JOELLE D. J. WICKENS, MATTHEW A. MICKLETZ, WILLIAM DONNELLY

All materials, man-made or otherwise, deteriorate over time. Preventive conservation refers to actions taken to slow this degradation by reducing the impact of the most common agents of deterioration: light, incorrect temperature and relative humidity, pollutants, pests, physical forces, fire, water, and disassociation. As we discuss in the pages that follow, there is much you can do at home to address these agents.

LIGHT

For light-sensitive objects, the only way to protect them from light damage is to keep them in the dark. Objects in the dark however, cannot be seen. Keeping a family treasure or purchasing an artwork only to pack it away in a closet is not likely to produce the pleasure we hope these objects will bring.

Natural and artificial light both produce three kinds of energy that can cause harm: ultraviolet, visible, and infrared. Singly or in combination, these energies cause objects to yellow, fade, shift from one color to another, and become dry and brittle. Objects in our home collections that are most at risk of this damage are textiles of any kind, photographs, paper, stained and/or varnished wooden furniture, and varnished paintings. But all is not lost! It is possible to reduce the damaging impact of light in a number of ways.

The use of framing glass that incorporates ultraviolet filters and the replacement of fluorescent, halogen, or incandescent (heat-generating) lightbulbs with LED varieties are two simple steps for eliminating ultraviolet radiation as well as reducing infrared (heat-generating) radiation and visible light. The protection of susceptible objects with tinted glass or Plexiglas and the use of semitransparent shades or tinted film on windows can also help.

Other simple steps you can take to reduce light damage include displaying an object for only a few months each year; hanging light-sensitive objects in rooms that are occupied less frequently or in rooms with no windows or skylights; and displaying objects outside any path of direct sunlight. In the end, you need to balance the desire to see objects (and therefore expose them to light) with the need to protect them from light damage. The intersection of these conflicting goals will determine how you display and store your light-sensitive treasures.

HUMIDITY AND TEMPERATURE

Personal preferences for how warm, cold, dry, or damp to keep a home can vary greatly. Geographic location and environmental considerations will also have an impact on the temperature and humidity of the spaces where you keep your treasured items. Despite this variability, there are some basic parameters that will help with protecting your objects from the damaging effects of incorrect temperature and relative humidity. When humidity levels fluctuate, objects with organic components (wood, paper, textiles) will expand and contract as they absorb and desorb moisture. How much of this fluctuation objects can handle varies with the type of object, and it's a challenge to define. If you hear furniture creaking, the joints may have loosened due to contraction of the wood in a dry month. Maybe you notice that loose photographs are curling or the finish on your dining room table is sticky. These are physical signs there is too little or too much moisture in the air.

An ambient or localized humidity level of 70 percent or above will generally promote mold growth. Objects on an exterior wall are at greater risk of mold because the space between the object and the wall can trap moisture. Objects near windows are also at greater risk due to temperature differentials on either side of the glass, which can create pockets of high humidity. Dusty objects are a third at-risk category, as dust will bind moisture to itself as well as to the object. On the other hand, particularly dry climates, with less than 30 percent relative humidity, can cause objects to become desiccated and brittle.

The higher the temperature, the faster that damaging chemical reactions will progress. A general rule of thumb is that for every 10°F/5°C you lower the temperature, you double the lifetime of an object. Storing objects at a temperature that is comfortable for humans is often all that is possible. Considering where it is colder in your house in a particular season and placing precious objects in those places can lengthen the life of an object. Care must be taken, however, to monitor humidity levels, as temperature and relative humidity are inversely dependent. As the temperature goes down, the relative humidity level will rise.

DUST/POLLUTANTS

Keep your collection as dust-free as possible. Dust is made up of many things, including hair, skin, lint, and particulate air pollutants such as sulfur and carbon. These elements, sitting on the surface of an object, can cause chemical deterioration of that surface (FIG. 1). Such elements also attract pests that will eat the dust as well as the object. Dust is hygroscopic by nature; it attracts and retains moisture, which creates a breeding ground for mold.

To slow this type of deterioration, objects that are displayed in the open should be dusted regularly. A wide variety of cloths and equipment is available (FIG. 2). The safest options for most collections include microfiber dust cloths, which are charged with static electricity and are dry and lint-free; long, fine-bristle brushes; and vacuum cleaners. Cloths treated with dust-attractant chemicals and chemicals designed to be sprayed on an object prior to dusting should be avoided. The likelihood of surface damage with these materials is extremely high.

FIG. 1 Areas with and without dust become obvious when seen in the raking light provided by a flashlight, which is a valuable tool when cleaning.

FIG. 2 Appropriate cleaning tools seen here include a soft-bristle hake brush; a white, woven microfiber dust cloth; and a yellow, nonwoven dust cloth treated with a trace amount of mineral oil.

You can test the effectiveness of a cloth by dusting a windowpane. Does the cloth remove and retain the dust? Does it leave the glass otherwise unchanged? A "yes" answer to these questions suggests that you have an effective dusting cloth. If dust remains behind or is dispersed in the air or there is evidence of oily residues left on the test surface, then your cloth is ineffective.

Be aware of surfaces that are too fragile to be dusted safely, such as those with flaking paint or crumbling gilded ornament. A careful examination of objects is wise before you set out on a dusting campaign. Long, soft-bristle brushes are particularly effective on fragile surfaces and in hard-to-reach areas, both of which are present on objects such as ornate, gilded frames (FIG. 3). It is best to dust *from* the object *onto* a dusting cloth rather than letting the dust float into the air, where it may be redeposited on objects nearby.

Vacuum cleaners are a more powerful approach to removing dust, but they must be used carefully. A standard household vacuum cleaner will work well on floors and around furniture; however, a system with controllable suction should be used on fragile objects such as aged

FIG. 3 Use a hake brush on a gilt surface to gently remove dust.

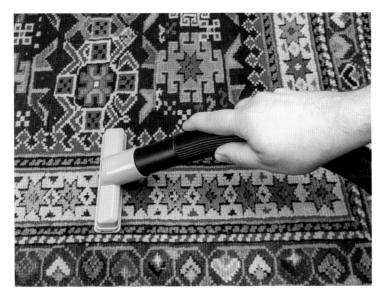

FIG. 4 A variable-speed HEPA-filtered vacuum can be used to carefully clean the fibers of a rug.

upholstery and rugs (FIG. 4). A soft mesh screen placed over the vacuum intake can prevent material from being sucked up and can reduce the risk of abrasion. Vacuum cleaners equipped with "HEPA" (High Efficiency Particulate Air) filters are capable of capturing very small particles and preventing the redistribution of dust. Whether you choose a standard

DUST UP CLOSE

The variety of materials within dust can be seen with examination at high magnification using a scanning electron microscope (SEM). This image of dust, taken at 236x magnification, shows the variety of shapes, sizes, and abrasiveness of materials commonly found in dust, including fibers, skin, minerals, and pollen (FIG. 5).

Minerals

Synthetic fiber

Skin

Pollen

Natural fiber

SEI MAG: 208 x HV: 10.0 kV WD: 8.9 mm Px: 0.79 µm

200 µm

FIG. 5 Secondary electron image of dust at 236x magnification annotated with visual identification of its components.

vacuum cleaner or one with HEPA filtration, remember that regular vacuuming is vital for both dust and insect control. In addition to dusting, additional options to protect objects from dust include proper filtering of heating and air-conditioning systems in the house; the placement of objects in acid-free boxes for storage; and the use of glass or acrylic cases for display.

PESTS

The word *pest* generally refers to rodents, birds, insects, and other types of animal life that pose a threat to the objects in your care. Taking measures to keep pests out of a space is an obvious, but often overlooked, precaution. Along with lighting, humidity, and dust control, reducing the risk of pest damage to vulnerable collections is critical. Storage areas such as attics and basements are often subject to unwanted visitors in the form of mice, birds, and bats. Insects are attracted to quiet, dark, unchecked spaces. Accumulated dust provides some insects with sufficient protein to sustain life. Dead insect carcasses are another life-sustaining location for some insects.

Maintaining proper collection hygiene is the first, and most important, step in pest control. Keeping food away from collections may be difficult at home, but creating unnecessary food debris, such as eating snacks while going through your old photograph collection, is asking for trouble. A clean area is the first line of defense (FIG. 6). Appropriate storage containers are the second. Metal and stable plastic units can help keep objects from getting soiled or chewed, whereas using shoeboxes to store grandmother's neatly folded love letters may result in tattered paper fragments recognizable as a mouse nest. Regular checking of stored and displayed objects is the third line of defense. If insect activity can be caught early, the damage will be significantly reduced.

Working with a professional pest control service may be the answer for some. It is best to find a firm that can control all types of animal life that are a potential risk for your collection. The company should also have a primary goal of protecting your items without pesticides. In general, spraying pesticides or setting off "bug bombs" around objects should be avoided. Passive measures ("sticky traps," light traps, sealing your building) should be adopted first. Request the use of snap traps for mice and rats rather than poison, which can leave dead rodents within your walls. Decaying carcasses are a food source that promotes pest activity inside the home.

FIG. 6 Inspecting objects for pest activity is key to helping stave off infestations and damage.

HANDLING

Before picking up an object, it is important to consider the object's needs. Should it be handled with gloves or with bare hands? Gloves should be worn when dealing with metal objects, since fingerprints can "etch" metallic surfaces and create intense tarnish known as lacunae. Gloves should also be worn when handling gilded surfaces or objects that have been inadvertently treated with pesticides. At the other end of the spectrum, gloves are problematic when picking up ceramics and glass, as manual dexterity is diminished with such objects, which tend to be slippery in nature. In all other cases, washed and completely dried hands are all that is required.

If you do wear gloves, powder-free nitrile gloves are preferred. Be sure to wash your hands immediately after removing them and before handling additional objects, as perspiration within the gloves is unavoidable. White cotton gloves are an option, but those can snag on fragile surfaces. They also soil quickly and can transfer soiling from one object to another. Avoid cotton gloves with PVC nubs, as tempting as they are for grip. They leave residue behind, which can cause damage, particularly to silver.

PACKING AND MOVING

Art handlers at Winterthur use utility carts and quilt-lined baskets for internal transport of objects within the museum. Items are nestled within cotton rags or sandbag weights to protect them from jostling. The packaging of objects for short-distance transport by staff involves a similar technique but with slightly different materials. Appropriate packing materials that are readily available for use at home include acid-free, unbuffered tissue paper, which protects the surface of the object; polyethylene bags, which envelop the object and provide protection from unexpected water damage; new brown cardboard boxes; and bubble wrap, which fills the voids and dampens vibration.

Note: Bubble wrap leaves impressions on painted surfaces and residue on other surfaces, so always place a protective layer between your object and the bubble wrap.

Before making any moves, it is important to have a plan. Where and how will the object be moved? Any related moves? For example, to retrieve a painting from an overmantel, should objects on the mantel be moved first? Are there any moveable parts on the object you intend to move? Lighting fixtures can have shades, hurricane globes, finials, and snuffers. Are there any old repairs that are weak or could be broken during handling? Ceramic handles and finials in particular tend to be areas of previous repair that are difficult to spot in regular light. Keep this in mind before moving the object.

For small frames, it is best to carry them by holding one of the sides as well as the bottom. Never carry a frame by the top; doing so could put undue strain on the corner joins, causing them to fail. With case furniture like dressers, the edges of drawer faces are often areas of previous repair. It can be tempting to open the drawer edge with your fingertips rather than using the drawer pull, but this could cause damage.

Professional crating can be expensive but is necessary for objects that need to travel great distances. If done well, crating can protect objects from damage by physical forces as well as fluctuations of temperature and humidity during transport. Objects should not, however, be stored long term within crates or moving boxes since the crating materials themselves could cause damage through the off-gassing of plasticizers in the foam, bubble wrap, or plastic bags. Packing boxes can also attract and become a home for silverfish, causing damage to paper-based objects and textiles.

STORAGE

Museum-grade storage materials are readily available online and may be called archival, buffered, unbuffered, or acid free, to name a few terms. It is important to consider the composition, durability, texture, and intended use of each before purchase. The following will help in making the appropriate choice.

ARCHIVAL

These materials are suitable for long-term contact with art or historic documents. They meet museum standards. Archival-quality mat boards made of cotton rag are used in framing works on paper. Non-archival mat board contains wood pulp, which oxidizes with age and causes discoloration along the edge of contact. This is known as mat burn and is not reversible.

ACID FREE OR BUFFERED

These materials contain an alkaline substance, usually calcium carbonate, which acts as a buffer from acids that could form as the storage material ages. Objects that are safe to store in contact with buffered materials include those made of cotton, flax, linen, jute, and other plant-based materials. Acid-free tissue paper, boxes, folders, envelopes, and mat board are all available.

UNBUFFERED

These materials are best for objects containing animal proteins, such as silk and wool, along with animal-based materials like natural history specimens, leather-bound books, and items containing pearl. If your treasured objects contain both cellulose and animal-based materials, unbuffered storage materials are preferred. Unbuffered tissue paper, file folders, envelopes, and boxes are all available.

RECORD KEEPING/DISSOCIATION

Good record keeping will prevent dissociation, which means separating an object from the intellectual knowledge that makes it significant. You should write down the history of your object, noting what makes it valuable. It may mean identifying people in family photographs, naming the makers of the sampler hanging on the wall, or documenting the name of the bride who wore the wedding dress. You should keep records of artists' names, purchase amounts, and appraisals by reliable sources.

Such information should be recorded in a way that allows it to be accessible for years to come. A computer inventory created on software that will become obsolete may not be the best option. Taking advantage of high-quality paper and pen may be the optimal solution. When possible, keeping documentation with the object is ideal, but do not tape or attach it any way that would cause damage to the object. In some cases, creating a second set of documents, kept in another location, many be worth the effort. This can be particularly helpful in the event of a fire or other emergency that damages or destroys your treasures.

EMERGENCY PREPAREDNESS

What constitutes an emergency differs greatly depending on geographical location and the type of structure involved. Whichever form, there is typically no doubt when the unexpected and extremely out-of-the-ordinary takes place. Awareness of what has the highest potential of causing damage to your collection is paramount, particularly broken water pipes, older electrical components/wiring, large trees near the structure, and clogged downspouts. You should be aware of what harsh weather events (tornadoes, hurricanes, earthquakes) are common to your area.

Advance planning can greatly reduce the amount of irreversible damage done to your objects should disaster strike. Proper storage is important, and having proper documentation will aide in the recovery process. A safe, secure place to keep documents, such as a fire-proof box, safe, or bank deposit box will be a lifesaver. Emergency supplies that should be located near your collection include plastic drop cloths, buckets, absorbent materials, paper towels, paper pulp mats and socks, a flashlight and extra batteries, pencil and paper, and a fire extinguisher. Other considerations include gloves, dust masks, hard hats, a reflective vest, and eye protection. In any emergency, however, it is important to remember that your safety and the safety of others should always be first and foremost.

WHEN TO CALL A PROFESSIONAL

Damage prevention is the best route to the long-term care of any collection. This chapter has introduced some basics for care, and the chapters that follow will address additional issues. In the end, however, you may need to call on a trained professional. Conservators spend many years studying both chemistry and art history. They share a common Code of Ethics and guidelines where treatments to your objects are to be well documented and reversible. They are your most important go-to source for advice. The American Institute for Conservation (AIC) is the professional organization for conservators in the

United States. Their website has a "find an expert" tool that supplies the names of those individuals who have trained in accredited programs and have been vetted as "professional associates." For more information, please visit www.culturalheritage.org.

FIG. 1 Family documents and ephemera can range from scrapbooks and letters to souvenir brochures and historic photos.

CHAPTER 2

Books, Documents, and Ephemera

MELISSA TEDONE

Our personal and family archives are filled with treasured books, printed and handwritten documents, ephemera, and digital files. These materials share the commonality of containing information important to us, whether visual, textual, or encoded. They also share the commonality of being composite objects made up of multiple materials, such as paper, ink, leather, cloth, plastics, and metals. As objects that are regularly handled and manipulated, books, documents, and ephemera are prone to a higher degree of deterioration from use than most artwork. They are also vulnerable to temperature and humidity fluctuations, which can cause their various materials to expand, contract, and warp. Fortunately, professional guidelines can help us handle and store these items safely while also using and enjoying them for years to come (FIG. 1).

GLOVES OR NO GLOVES?

Television documentaries often show readers wearing white cotton gloves while handling archives documents or turning the pages of rare books. While this was the norm at one point, conservators and librarians no longer recommend wearing gloves for handling most books and documents. Gloves reduce tactile sensitivity and can snag on fragile page edges, ultimately doing more harm than good. The best approach is to wash and dry hands thoroughly and then resist the urge to put on hand lotion before handling objects. The one exception to this glove guideline is when handling photographs, which are far more vulnerable to damage from the natural oils on our skin than other paper-based items.

NATURE OF THE MATERIALS

BOOKS

Structurally, books are the most complex objects in this chapter. A book's structure may be as humble as a stapled pamphlet or as luxurious as a gold-tooled, leather-bound book sewn on raised bands. Regardless, both ends of the spectrum may be highly prized as cultural artifacts and must continue to function as intended. Common materials found in books include paper, printer's ink, decorative papers, adhesives, leather, parchment, fabric, hemp cord, and thread. This mixed collection of materials that we call the book must be able to flex and provide support throughout the structure for the volume to function (FIG. 2). Problems occur when one or more of the materials in a book become weak or rigid. Then the covers may fall off; the pages may loosen or detach; and the paper may tear. External forces, such as a book accidentally getting wet, may affect the different materials in different ways, leading to stains, straining, and breakage. Internal forces, such as acidic compounds in the paper and leather and corrosive media may also be at work.

HANDWRITTEN AND PRINTED DOCUMENTS

Manuscripts and documents are composed of paper or parchment leaves inscribed with printed and handwritten ink and may be adorned with seals, ribbons, and postal stamps. They are often creased, torn, and soiled from a postal journey or everyday wear-and-tear, or faded from display. In addition, the acidic, iron-based ink that was in common use from the eighth century through the opening decades of the twentieth century often corrodes and weakens the paper around it.

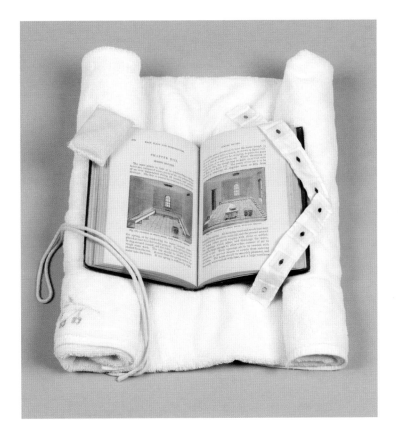

FIG. 2 The expensive, foam book wedges found in rare book libraries to safely support treasured books are not a necessary investment for the home collection. A clean, dry, cotton towel can be rolled into a soft support that cradles an open book just as effectively. Light weights may also be used to help the pages stay open.

Writing inks age more unpredictably than printing inks, because recipes for writing inks over time have been so variable, both before and after the commercial manufacture of inks began during the Industrial Revolution. Modern writing inks are proprietary, so industry secrets make it challenging to understand their components and how they might age. Most printing inks found in books tend to be relatively stable, although high oil content can migrate into adjacent paper, creating a "halo" around the text or offset onto adjacent pages, particularly if books are stored in fluctuating environmental conditions. Printing inks used for ephemera, especially color inks, can be especially vulnerable to light and humidity damage.

EPHEMERA

The term ephemera usually refers to printed documents that were originally intended for short-term use, such as souvenirs or items of historical interest. These materials, because they were not produced with an eye toward longevity and durability, often suffer from inherent vice. By this we mean that the very nature of their materials leads to inevitable deterioration. Ephemera may include advertisements, cigar boxes, baseball and trade cards, broadsides, event programs, calendars, brochures, greeting cards, postcards, menus, paper dolls, and postage stamps.

If you are fortunate enough to have newspaper clippings that predate the 1850s in your collection, then they are likely in stable condition, since acidic wood pulp papers were not manufactured widely until the mid-nineteenth century. Most ephemera, however, including newspapers from the second half of the nineteenth century and later, are printed on inexpensive, wood-pulp paper. Such papers are a prime example of inherent vice and are best stored safely away from heat, light, and dust. Encapsulating fragile wood pulp papers between layers of polyester film allows them to be handled safely.

SCRAPBOOKS

Scrapbooks may be homemade structures or commercially sold blank books with contents added by the creator or consumer. Sometimes these blank books are marketed specifically for scrapbook use and have flexible binding structures that are made to accommodate the additional bulk of the items added to them. Many historical scrapbooks, however, were made by repurposing a book that was not originally intended for this use. Scrapbooks are therefore often physically fragile and full of inherent vice. Their binding structures are compromised by their contents, which can cause physical strain to the bindings and may be chemically incompatible with adjacent materials. For example, highly acidic dried plant materials, such as pressed flowers, will cause oxidation of the cellulose on facing papers, leaving a "burn" pattern.

Scrapbooks present some of the most difficult challenges in the preservation world. They require special care and consideration every time they are opened. Covers must be supported to avoid stress on the binding (FIG. 3). Pages must be turned slowly, and support must be provided for loose or detached items. Fragile, detached items can be placed in labeled envelopes, with a note about their original location in the book. The use of a book box that is rigid and strong

FIG. 3 A smartphone scanner app used over a properly supported book is a far safer copy option than scanning a book on a flatbed scanner or photocopier, which can damage the binding.

enough to support and protect the scrapbook is imperative for any preservation effort. Ideally, all scrapbooks should be maintained intact, since a significant part of their value lies in the arrangement of pages by their creator. When the structure or contents are too physically fragile or chemically vulnerable to maintain in their original state, a conservation professional can suggest alternatives.

OVERSIZE MATERIALS

Maps, design drawings, and blueprints are often oversize and present special challenges. Maps vary from folded road maps to large wall maps mounted on muslin and rolled around a wooden bar. Design drawings that document structures, transportation equipment, landscapes, and the work of decorative arts and industrial craftsmen might be executed in pencil, ink, or watercolor on paper, tracing paper, and drafting cloth. Blueprint is often used as a generic term for many different photo-reproductive processes that vary widely in appearance and stability, although true blueprints are actually oversize cyanotype photographs. In spite of their varied components, oversize materials share two defining characteristics that create special preservation problems: their size makes safe handling and storage difficult, and their past function as working documents often exposed them to heavy use, light, and dirt.

    Whenever possible, oversize materials should be stored flat in archival-quality folders and/or interleaved with archival-quality paper.

Maps and design drawings can be gently unfolded or unrolled if they are strong enough. With material that is partially folded, try to avoid cross-folds. If the material is brittle, torn, or resistant to flattening, seek the advice of a conservator.

When flat storage is impossible, rolled storage is the alternative. Many oversize maps and drawings have already been tightly rolled and may have suffered tears, creases, and distortion. If they are still reasonably flexible, their condition can be improved by gently rolling them around a rigid tube that is four to six inches in diameter. Archival-quality tubes can be purchased from numerous vendors. Alternatively, a carpet tube can be covered with an isolation layer of polyester film, followed by a layer of archival-quality paper. The map or drawing can then be gently rerolled onto the lined tube. Once rolled, cover the outside of the map or drawing with a layer of archival-quality paper loosely tied with a flat cotton twill tape to protect from light and dust.

MACHINE-READABLE & DIGITAL MEDIA

The preservation of machine-readable and digital media is a growing area of research, as our VHS tapes, audiocassettes, and digital files stored on CD, DVD, and computer hard drives prove increasingly vulnerable. What all these types of media have in common is the need for some sort of device in order to access the information they contain, but both media and playback equipment can become obsolete.

Digital records are particularly vulnerable because any deterioration means the loss is catastrophic. For example, most of a damaged book may still be readable even if a few pages are torn out and lost, but when digital information becomes corrupted, the entire file is unreadable. The physical components (plastics, paperboard, metals, etc.) of these materials benefit from the same care applied to other home documents, such as protection from light, heat, humidity fluctuations, and dust.

Make sure that file names do not contain any spaces, and do not use periods in a file name except where they occur right before the file extension code.

Vulnerable file names: Important Document.pdf
Important.document. pdf

Best practice file names: ImportantDocument.pdf
Important_Document.pdf

You should save important documents as PDFs for the long term. They are a more stable file format than MS Word. Store photos as hi-resolution TIFFs and use lower-resolution jpgs for sharing online and posting to social media. The highest resolution needed for most computer screens is 72ppi, but 300ppi is required for a crisp printed image.

Keep multiple copies of the most important files in multiple places. In addition to a local hard drive, consider using online "cloud" storage services. It is important to remember, however, that so-called "cloud" storage actually refers to physical computer servers, usually stored in massive warehouses in remote locations. The long-term reliability of these servers depends on the resources and commitment of the company that maintains them. You should avoid relying on flash or jump drives for long-term storage; they are built as transportation devices only.

Research into best preservation practices for these materials continues to advance rapidly, so the safest option is to monitor the websites of organizations known to be leaders in this area: the Library of Congress, the National Archives, the Association of Moving Image Archivists (AMIA), the Digital Preservation Coalition (DPC), the National Digital Stewardship Alliance (NDSA), and the Open Preservation Foundation (OPF).

WHAT YOU CAN DO

Preventive care that includes clean and safe storage can have an enormous impact on the longevity of family archives. Appropriate protective boxes, sleeves, and folders can provide physical support and protect items from dust and light. Enclosures can also create microclimates, which buffer the items inside from small fluctuations in temperature and humidity. Storage materials should be stable, archival-

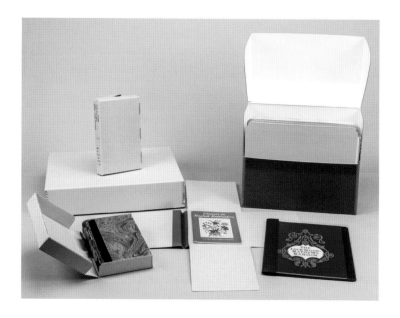

FIG. 4 Affordable, commercially available enclosures for books and documents can be an easy and effective way to preserve your collection.

quality papers, cardboards, book cloths, and plastics that will not deteriorate with time or damage the objects that they enclose (FIG. 4).

When purchasing commercially made storage products for documents, ephemera, and books, keep in mind that the term archival does not have a legal definition in the United States, so manufacturers can use the word without discretion. Look instead for the terms acid-free and lignin-free on paper products. Acid-free products are pH neutral when they leave the manufacturing plant but can still become acidic over time if they contain lignin (a component of wood pulp). Lignin-free papers and boards are therefore likely to be a more reliable option for the long term. Buffered refers to papers and boards impregnated with alkaline salts that can absorb acids from their environments for some period of time. Buffered storage materials are safe for most paper-based items, with the exception of true blueprints and other photographs, which are sensitive to high pH and should always be stored in a neutral environment.

Stable plastic products are those made from polyester, polyethylene, or polypropylene. Avoid plastics made with polyvinyl chloride (PVC), which can emit harmful chlorine and leach sticky plasticizers. Polyester films should be avoided when storing drawings in charcoal, pastel, or

FIGS. 5A, B (A) Books may be damaged by improper shelving that causes them to slump or lean. Pulling a book off the shelf by its headcap can damage the spine. (B) Properly shelved, well-supported books will age better than books shelved haphazardly. Carefully removing a book from the shelf by gripping the boards will protect the vulnerable spine.

any other loose media since the static charge of the film can pull the drawing material off the paper.

The shelving or drawers used to store your collection should also be composed of stable materials (FIGS. 5A, B). The most readily available storage furniture is powder-coated or archival-quality baked enamel steel. These coating processes ensure that the furniture will not give off damaging solvent vapors, which can happen with wooden furniture, particularly in a closed environment such as a drawer or bookcase. If wooden furniture must be used, it should be coated with a stable, properly cured resin recommended by a conservation professional, or it should be lined with a layer of archival-quality paper and plastic. Good air circulation is also important for storage areas, to avoid buildup of indoor air pollution, mold, and humidity (FIGS. 5A, B).

Heavily soiled materials should be cleaned before they are stored. Books in otherwise stable condition can be cleaned by holding them firmly closed while lightly brushing away dust with a clean, dry, soft-bristle brush or by vacuuming the edges of the text and outside covers with a vacuum attachment covered with cheesecloth. Conduct cleaning in a well-ventilated area. Avoid skin contact and minimize inhalation of dust by wearing long sleeves, gloves, and an N95 disposable respirator, available at any hardware store.

Do not vacuum moldy items with a household vacuum, as this will only spread spores throughout the air. Mold is a health hazard and causes irreparable damage to paper if left unchecked. We interact intimately with books. As we handle them, the movement of the pages and the close proximity of our face as we read means that we may be breathing in a higher percentage of mold spores than we do in ambient air. For actively moldy books that must be kept, prompt consultation with a professional is essential.

WHEN TO CALL A PROFESSIONAL

Papers and inks can have complicated chemistry, so contact a conservator rather than applying sprays or coatings to brittle or darkening paper. Although hobby and craft stores sell aerosol spray products that claim to de-acidify documents, newspapers, and other paper-based materials, these sprays are a non-reversible treatment that can cause inks to bleed and change the surface characteristics of the paper. They are also a temporary fix at best, so the risk is rarely worth it. Consult a professional before making any repair with pressure-sensitive tapes or adhesives on books and other paper-based items. Sometimes, commercially available repair products can worsen deterioration, making conservation treatment more difficult and costly later. Conservators can salvage books or other paper items that have gotten wet, mend torn documents, rebind deteriorating volumes, and offer advice on preventive preservation strategies (FIG. 6).

FIG. 6 Consult a professional before attempting to repair books or documents using DIY methods. Conservators apply a thorough historical and scientific understanding of materials, specialized craft skills, and a professional code of ethics to every object they examine or conserve.

THE SCIENCE OF INK

Have you ever seen old, handwritten documents with holes in the paper in areas of the text? These holes are the result of the slow deterioration of the iron gall ink that subsequently "eats" its way through the paper. Iron gall ink is a ubiquitous historical ink composed of tannins (most often extracted from gall nuts or bark), vitriol (a mixture of iron and other metal salts), natural tree gums, and water. Iron gall ink has been in use since the first century CE.

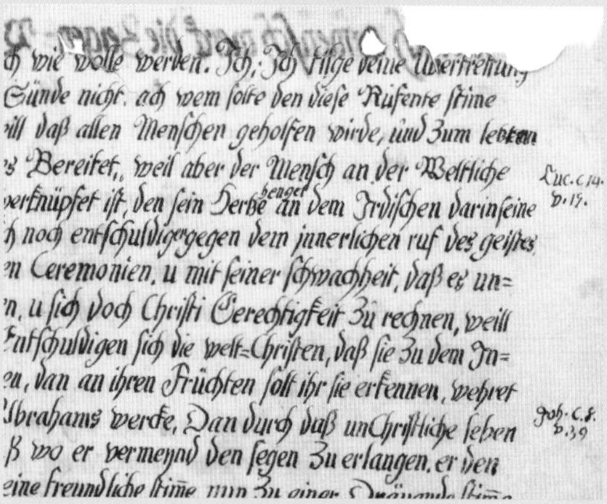

FIG. 7 This manuscript shows the areas where iron gall ink has caused holes and where the ink has penetrated through the paper.

The chemical degradation of iron gall ink on paper is complex and not fully understood, despite more than a century of research on the topic. The destructive nature of some iron gall inks on paper is due to multiple factors, including the natural aging of paper, the composition of the ink, and the reactivity of the ink with the media (the natural gums and water). The degree of degradation is influenced by a lifetime of exposure to fluctuating temperatures and humidity as well as the presence of additives in the paper itself. Scientists continue to research iron gall ink degradation and collaborate with conservators to develop methods capable of impeding or, hopefully, halting its destruction of paper.

FIG. 1 This extraordinary Chinese birdcage dating from the early 1800s is a good example of different organic materials used in combination. The ribs and feet are tortoiseshell; the base is bamboo and wood; the feeder and decorative plaque are carved from ivory; and the perch is a tree branch with bone collars at either end. The cage sustained damage over the years but has been conserved and has since remained in good condition.

CHAPTER 3

Organic Materials

LARA KAPLAN

Readily available in the environment, organic materials have been used worldwide for millennia to create objects of art and daily life. They are made from the once-living tissues of plants and animals. Synthetically produced rubbers and plastics also fall under this category, since they, too, are organic in nature. Organic materials are found in collections of all types, whether they are fine and decorative arts, objects from indigenous cultures, modern and contemporary art, or natural history specimens. Some are more prone to deterioration than others but with proper care can be maintained in good condition for many years (FIG. 1).

PLANT MATERIALS

The basic building block of plant materials is cellulose, a complex carbohydrate that forms plant cell walls. Many species of plants are well suited for creating art and artifacts. Their roots, stems, wood, branches, leaves, bark, and even seeds have unique properties that can serve wide-ranging uses. Basketry is quite common, but many other types of objects can be made as well: tools, containers, musical instruments, sculptures, and ornaments, to name a few.

After harvesting, some degree of processing is generally necessary before plant materials can be fashioned into objects. For example, leaves and stems can be soaked and heated to soften them, remove extraneous compounds, or aid in extracting fibers. Wood can be split into long, thin splints for weaving. Colors can be changed through sun-bleaching or dyeing, with the final appearance of an object further altered with paints and other finishes. Although they serve an important purpose, many of these processes compromise the long-term stability of the plant materials.

Objects made of plant materials vary in their sensitivity. A sturdy wood sculpture may need nothing more than a stable environment and periodic dusting to remain in good condition. Baskets and other items made of finer, thinner materials, are more susceptible to damage (FIG. 2). They may exhibit discoloration and embrittlement as they degrade and acidify from exposure to air, light, and cycling relatively humidity.

FIG. 2 This 1930s Mohawk basket made of ash splints and sweetgrass shows many common condition concerns. The ash splints were originally dyed a vibrant pinkish-red, which is visible where the lid protected the basket from light. On the exposed exterior, however, the dye has faded completely, and the ash has darkened to a deep brown. The ash is now brittle, causing the delicate decorative twists projecting from the sides to be easily broken. Ingrained dust and dirt on the lid give it a grayish cast, especially on the top surface.

Pliable materials can stiffen and become impossible to flex without cracking or breaking. Dirt and dust can easily become trapped within porous surfaces or the interstices of a weave and be difficult to remove. Soft baskets can collapse under their own weight, and objects hung by their handles or other vulnerable areas can eventually break from the prolonged tension. Proper support and display strategies are key in these kinds of situations. A common past practice was to "feed" baskets with waxes or oils. Although this may temporarily restore sheen, it should be avoided, since it confers no long-term benefit and may cause new problems as the applied materials themselves deteriorate.

SKIN AND LEATHER

Many materials can be made from the skin and internal soft tissues of animals. Rawhide, parchment, leather, and fur are skin-based. Gutskin—a thin, translucent material—is made from intestinal linings. Strands of sinew (tendon) are used to make thread and cordage. All these materials consist primarily of the protein collagen, which forms networks of microscopic fibers that give skin and other soft tissues their characteristic strength and flexibility.

Any number of techniques can transform the raw material into durable products. Rawhide, a rigid and tough material, requires little more than careful cleaning, scraping, and drying under tension to create, but it remains highly sensitive to moisture.

This is in large part due to the crucial step of *tanning*, where the protein structure of skin is chemically altered by soaking in a tanning solution. Various tanning methods have been used throughout history to create different types of leather. One of the most common is vegetable tanning, an ancient technique found the world-over that utilizes plant extracts (tannins) as the tanning agent. The vast majority of modern leather is made by chrome tanning, a form of mineral tanning developed in the late nineteenth century. Faster, cheaper, and producing a more resistant leather, it quickly replaced vegetable tanning shortly after it was introduced.

Skin, leather, and related materials are especially vulnerable to the ravages of time. The main culprits are oxygen, light, and pollutants, which lead to weakening, stiffening, and embrittlement. Some leathers, especially vegetable-tanned leathers from the mid- to late nineteenth century, undergo acidic changes, also known as *red rot*, which significantly worsens their deterioration (FIG. 3). As they age, skin and leather items that were once flexible can take on permanent folds or deformations, and weight-bearing components may no longer be

FIG. 3 During the Industrial Revolution, changes in leather processing gave rise to leathers that are highly prone to developing red rot, especially when kept in environments with high levels of airborne pollutants. Leather with this condition will easily abrade, crack, tear, and develop a reddish, powdery surface, as can be seen in this aged chair upholstery. Conservators are currently researching treatment approaches to address red rot.

structurally sound. Similar to baskets, proper support and mounts are needed to prevent damage (FIG. 4). Once deteriorated, all skin materials will be susceptible to water damage, no matter how they were originally processed. Repeated wetting can wash out tanning agents and also cause staining, hardening, and shrinkage. Insect damage is a concern as well, especially for furs or other items that still have hair.

FIG. 4 A custom-made padded brass mount is necessary to safely display this vegetable-tanned leather pouch and an attached powder horn, which date from the mid-1700s to early 1800s. The antler-handle knife is a later addition. The leather is extremely fragile, and the straps are no longer able to support the pouch and other components. The mount takes the weight off the straps, allowing the ensemble to be hung on a wall without risking breakage.

As with "feeding" baskets, there is a popular misconception that applying leather dressings will keep leather objects strong and supple. Such a process may be beneficial for new objects in active use, but it can cause irreversible damage on historic objects since the components of these products break down over time, especially if they have been applied excessively. Surfaces can become dark and sticky or harden and flake off, and a white haze (called a *bloom* or *spew*) can develop and be difficult to remove. Leather in good condition is best left alone.

HORN, TORTOISESHELL, AND FEATHERS

Structures arising from the outer layer of skin are common in the animal kingdom. Some, like horn, tortoiseshell, hooves, and claws, are hard and tough; others are softer and more flexible, such as hair, feathers, and porcupine quills. Although outwardly different, they are all made of keratin, a strong and resilient protein.

In addition to its toughness and stability, keratin is thermoplastic, meaning that it becomes malleable with heat and will retain a new shape upon cooling. This useful property allows keratinous materials, especially the harder varieties, to be pressed or molded into different forms. Horn can be flattened into sheets and cut into panels, veneers, and buttons or shaped into spoons, cups, and innumerable other utilitarian and decorative objects.

Tortoiseshell (which despite the name is obtained from sea turtles) is similar to horn in its working properties and uses, but its rarity and beautiful pigmentation patterns have made it a more expensive material, historically reserved for luxury goods. An early goal of the plastics industry was to imitate costly materials such as tortoiseshell. Some faux tortoiseshell looks just like the real thing but has very different ageing properties, so it is important to identify properly. Horn and tortoiseshell are relatively durable, but they are still sensitive to environmental fluctuations and can warp and crack, especially if cut into thin veneers that are constrained, as may be the case with inlays or linings.

Highly decorative in form and color, feathers are a popular choice for accessories such as hats, bags, and jewelry. They have many practical purposes too, such as pen quills, dusters, arrow fletching, and fans. Feathers become increasingly fragile over time and can easily crease or break. Fading of light-sensitive pigments and dyes is another serious concern. Feathers and other soft keratinous materials are also extremely prone to insect damage. Despite their toughness, horn and tortoiseshell can be readily attacked as well (FIG. 5).

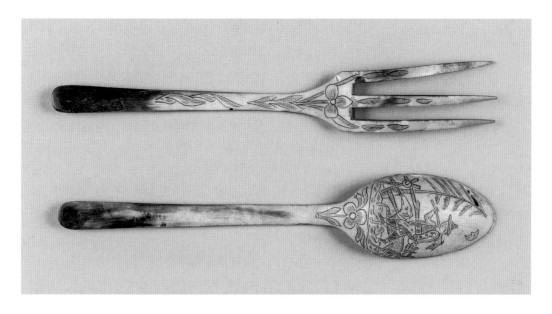

FIG. 5 Carpet beetles are the likely culprits for the irregular losses on this serving fork and spoon set with decorative engraving. Additionally, a large loss near the base of one of the tines on the fork made it vulnerable to deformation in response to changes in temperature and relative humidity; it has therefore lifted away from its neighboring tines.

IVORY, BONE, AND SHELL

Skeletal materials such as ivory and bone are composed of calcium-containing minerals embedded in a collagen matrix, a combination that provides both strength and resiliency. Ivory comes from teeth or tusks, which are simply elongated teeth. Elephant ivory, like tortoiseshell, has been valued as a high-end material, but ivories from other animals such as walrus, whale, and hippo are also commonly used. Teeth grow in distinct layers and are dense and fine-grained. Bones tend to be more structurally uniform and are generally more porous to allow for the passage of tiny blood vessels. Each can be used to make a wide variety of objects, from humble sewing needles to ornately carved sculptures.

Ivory and bone will both expand and contract in response to changes in relative humidity. Ivory is at higher risk of cracking because of its layered structure, but both are vulnerable if movement is restricted (FIG. 6). Surfaces can bleach from light exposure. They can also darken or yellow due to oxidation of oils and other organic constituents. This type of patina is often

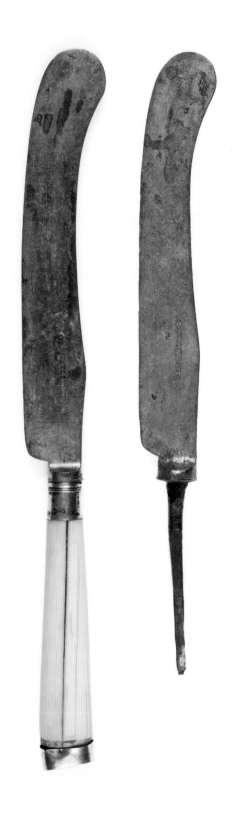

FIG. 6 The ivory handle on this dinner knife from the 1700s, made by the British firm Savery and Pryor, has cracked due to restricted movement. A steel tang on the inside kept the ivory from contracting in response to low relative humidity, and a silver ferrule and cap on the outside prevented it from expanding when the relative humidity was higher. The second knife is missing its handle completely, giving a good view of the steel tang.

considered desirable for older pieces and may even be mimicked with a dye or coating. Ivory especially can benefit from being displayed or stored in a case or cabinet, which will protect it from light and environmental changes.

Shell is made mostly of calcium carbonate with only a small amount of organic material. It forms the protective exoskeletons of various invertebrates, such as mollusks and snails. Shell is often used decoratively, as in jewelry and inlays, but can also be incorporated into tools and utensils. While less sensitive to environmental changes than ivory or bone, shell can react with air pollutants—specifically sulfur dioxide from car exhaust and volatile organic acids released from certain types of wood—and develop a powdery surface, a condition called *Byne's efflorescence* that can be quite destructive over time. Storage in wooden drawers or cabinets should therefore be avoided. If a shell surface does become compromised, contact a professional conservator to assess the problem and recommend appropriate corrective actions.

RUBBERS AND PLASTICS

The earliest industrially manufactured rubbers and plastics began as chemically modified natural materials. Vulcanized rubber was invented in the 1840s, followed by cellulose nitrate in the 1860s and cellulose acetate in the 1890s. The first fully synthetic plastic, phenol formaldehyde (Bakelite), was patented around 1910. Many of today's familiar plastics, such as acrylics (Lucite and Plexiglas), polyvinyl chloride (vinyl), polyurethane, polyethylene, and polyester, were developed during World War I and II, with others following over the course of the twentieth century. Plastics can be produced as molded forms, sheets, foams, fibers, films, and coatings, making them incredibly versatile. As a result, they are ubiquitous in everyday objects, jewelry, and collectibles and find frequent use in modern and contemporary art.

It is a common misconception that plastics will last forever. Although some are more stable than others, they will all degrade eventually. How and when this happens depends on the type of plastic in question and the specific additives it contains. Discoloration, stickiness, deformation,

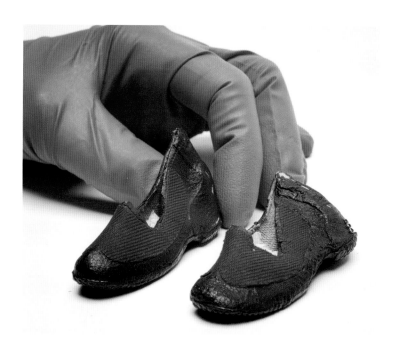

FIG. 7 These miniature over-shoes, likely dating to the late nineteenth century, were made in large quantities as sales models for the Boston Rubber Shoe Company. They are coated on the outside with a thin film of vulcanized rubber that has hardened and is starting to crack. Deformations, likely resulting from poor storage, cannot be reshaped without causing further damage.

embrittlement, cracking, and splitting are all signs that a plastic is deteriorating (FIG. 7). The conservation of plastics remains an evolving area, as deterioration mechanisms become better understood and new treatment strategies are developed. Keeping plastics in a cool, dark, stable environment will help increase their lifespan. Many plastics in good condition can be safely cleaned with water and a soft cloth, but even this may be damaging. It is therefore best to consult a conservator to determine the best course of action.

WHAT YOU CAN DO

Organic materials may differ widely in form and composition, but they share traits that make them environmentally sensitive.

They are porous and hygroscopic to varying degrees, meaning they readily take on and release water vapor, expanding in humid conditions and contracting when the air is dry. Dramatic fluctuations in relative humidity can result in warping, cracking, and breakage, especially if an object's movement is somehow constrained. *Keeping relative humidity levels stable will help avoid this kind of damage.*

Heat can also be an issue. In addition to speeding up rates of chemical deterioration, high temperatures can lead to embrittlement in dry environments and mold growth in humid ones. *Organic materials are therefore best kept in environments with cool temperatures and moderate relative humidity levels.*

Porosity makes organic materials prone to absorbing fine dust and pollutants from the air, potentially causing discoloration and adverse chemical reactions. *When practical, keeping objects displayed in cases or covered when not on view will help by preventing dust from building up in the first place. Objects with stable surfaces can be lightly dusted with a soft brush, but consult a conservator if the object is too delicate for dusting or requires more involved cleaning.*

All organic materials are sensitive to light, especially the ultraviolet radiation in sunlight and many forms of artificial light. Light damage can manifest as visual changes, such as bleaching and fading or darkening and discoloration, depending on the materials involved. It can also lead to structural breakdown, contributing to overall weakening and disintegration. *As much as possible, keep organic materials out of direct light.*

Many organic materials are also vulnerable to damage from insects and other pests. Powdery residues (frass), casings, and irregular losses are all signs of an infestation. Some insects, such as powder post beetles, eat cellulose found in plant materials. Webbing clothes moths, carpet beetles, and other protein-eating digesting insects can damage objects made of animal materials. Dust, dirt, and moisture make organic materials more readily digestible to pests of all kinds. *Keeping objects clean and dry will reduce the chances of an infestation occurring. A great deal of damage can happen quickly, so regular monitoring is crucial. If an active infestation is suspected, isolate the affected object by sealing it in a plastic bag and contact a conservator immediately.*

USING SCIENCE TO CLASSIFY ORGANICS

A very important technique for the identification of organic materials is Fourier-transform infrared spectroscopy (FTIR). In this process, infrared radiation interacts with a sample to give information on specific groups of atoms that make up organic molecules. Therefore, FTIR is particularly useful for classifying organic materials such as leather, paint medium, or plastic as well as previous repairs made with adhesives or coating. With information gained from FTIR, a conservator can choose the appropriate methods of treating the object.

FIG. 8 The hair comb on the left was made by Day, Clark, & Co. in Newark, New Jersey, between 1895–1935; the hair comb on the right is probably from the early to mid-20th century. They may appear to be made from similar materials, but FTIR tells a different story.

Upon visual examination, these combs look like they are both made from tortoiseshell. When tested using FTIR, however, we found that the comb on the right is actually imitation tortoiseshell, made from a plastic, cellulose nitrate. With this information, conservators can make informed decisions about the care, storage, and treatment of these two materially different combs.

CHAPTER 4

Ceramics and Glass

LAUREN FAIR

Objects made of ceramics and glass come from the clay and mineral deposits in the ground below us and in the natural world around us— from the aluminum, silicon, and iron in our soils to the salt in our oceans and potassium in our forests. Ceramics and glass as material classes are often grouped together because of their similarity in material makeup. They also both require the use of extreme heat in the form of kiln firing or furnace working in order to be made into the precious objects we collect for display, use, and enjoyment in our homes and institutions.

VULNERABILITIES OF CERAMICS AND GLASS

When we think of objects made of ceramics and glass, the number one vulnerability that might come to mind is breakage. We have all had that moment when we dropped something and waited that split-second for the inevitable, excruciating crash (FIGS. 1A, B). Hopefully, the object was replaceable or you knew a conservator to call.

The devastation of breaking ceramics and glass is one type of *physical* damage that can occur. Ceramic and glass objects can also crack and break for other reasons, such as the thermal shock that occurs when pouring hot tea in a ceramic mug that has been outside on a cold day. Because of the way ceramic and glass objects are made, they can inherently contain built-up stresses inside their structures. Think of a ceramic

FIGS. 1A, B The flare rim of this blue glass vase was accidentally knocked into, causing significant breakage. Conservation-grade adhesive is used here to reassemble the glass.

that is made by forming wet clay on a spinning wheel or of a gather of molten glass being spun on a blow pipe. The molecules in both cases are being forced to align in certain ways, and then, in the case of the ceramic, they are dried out and fired in place; in the case of the glass, they are cooled in place. If the drying out, firing, or cooling happens for too long, not long enough, or is done too quickly, stresses can build up within the body of the ceramic or glass that make it even more vulnerable to breakage. If bumped in the right way, a ceramic or glass object may crack or break entirely, even if the bump did not seem hard enough to cause that kind of damage (FIGS. 1A, B). In rare cases, a ceramic or glass object may break or crack spontaneously while sitting on a shelf.

Other forms of physical damage include scratching and abrasion, which often result in the loss of decoration layers. Common forms of decoration on ceramics include colored slips (dilute clay) and glazes, and common forms of decoration on both ceramics and glass include enamels (colored glass fused atop the glass or glazed ceramic) and gilding. Although not as common, ceramics and glass may also be decorated with "cold" paint and gilding, which means these decoration layers are not fired on and are even more at risk of loss by abrasion.

Regarding their *chemical* vulnerabilities, ceramic and glass objects are generally stable with regard to changes in the environment; however, there are a few exceptions. For one, exposure to acids, such as acidic foods, can cause a chemical breakdown of the surface of a glass or glazed ceramic. In the case of ceramics, and depending on the porosity (porous earthenware vs. non-porous hard-paste porcelain), disfiguring staining material can enter through crazing (a fine network of cracks in the glaze) and penetrate a porous ceramic body. Also with porous ceramics, salt permeation can be a vulnerability (FIGS. 2A, B). Certain salts, such as sodium chloride (table salt), can enter a porous ceramic when dissolved in water. Upon drying, the salts will crystallize, thereby growing in size and causing physical pressure within the body of

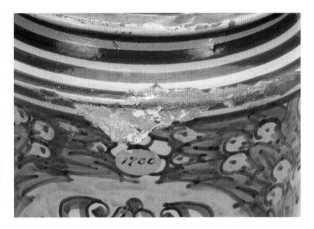

FIGS. 2A, B This tin-glazed earthenware apothecary jar once contained dry stuffs likely used for medicinal purposes. The contents have migrated into the porous earthenware body through flaws or losses in the glaze, and, over time, soluble salt components have changed shape and caused physical damage to the glaze layer. In this case, the salt contamination is directly related to what was stored in the container.

the ceramic. This is the same phenomenon that happens with salt crystallization in the exterior walls of stone and brick architecture and can sometimes cause extreme forms of flaking, spalling, and breakage of the ceramic and decoration layers.

GLASS DISEASE

Glass (including glazes on ceramics) has a particular chemical vulnerability that is unique to this class of materials. Made up of an interlocking network of primarily silicon and oxygen atoms, glass additionally contains fluxes and stabilizers such as lead, sodium, calcium, potassium, and/or magnesium, which help make the glass usable and stable. The deterioration phenomenon known as "glass disease" occurs when the ratios of those materials that make up the glass are disproportionate to one another so that they are not adequately tied up in the network. They can consequently leach out of the glass over time, coming to the surface and creating voids in the body of the glass. Glass with this condition can often be referred to as *sick* or *weeping glass*, as the components are literally weeping from the matrix.

Glass disease can also occur in "healthy" glass that has a fine balance in its chemical makeup but has been exposed to particularly harsh environments or cycles of environmental extremes. One common place this can happen is in the household dishwasher. Do *not* put precious glass or ceramic objects in the dishwasher! The harsh chemicals and extreme temperatures inside a typical machine will leach

FIG. 3 Here we see glasses exhibiting two different stages of deterioration: (*left*) early-stage, where the glass is made permanently hazy, possibly from repeated cleaning in a dishwasher; and (*right*) later-stage, with "full-on crizzling," where the glass matrix has been broken up and components have leached from the surface, causing a fine network of readily visible cracks.

components out of the glass over repeated exposures, leaving voids in the body of the glass, much like what happens in sick glass.

In either case, glass with glass disease can range from cloudy in appearance, which does not go away when washed (FIG. 3, *left*), to extremely "crizzled," exhibiting a fine network of cracks throughout (FIG. 3, *right*). In the most extreme cases, glass becomes crizzled to such an extent that it appears nearly opaque and begins to break apart. Unfortunately, none of these condition issues are reversible, and the best course of action for glass with glass disease is to place it in a controlled environment (see Handling and Storage, below).

RESTORATIONS

Because breakage is the number one vulnerability of ceramic and glass objects, reassembly and repair are the most common forms of restoration for historical ceramic and glass collections. Some of the earliest repairs ever discovered include drilled holes and pieces joined with lead staples or leather lashings. Early adhesives include bitumen, shellac, various tree resins, and animal glues. In modern history, metal staples and rivets of all kinds have been used (FIG. 4), and common adhesives include

FIG. 4 This mochaware teapot has copper alloy staples drilled partially into the underside of the lid to repair it. While unsightly, these repairs can render a ceramic water-tight, avoiding the need for any adhesive.

epoxy, cellulose nitrate, and "white glues," which are typically polyvinyl acetate (PVA) adhesives. None of these joining methods age well. At worst, they cause additional damage to the mended objects over time.

One of the biggest areas of research in the professional conservation field today is adhesives. Conservators now have at their disposal many excellent materials to choose from depending on the type of ceramic or glass, the nature of its damage, and the precise strength a particular repair may require. Most important, years of testing, research, and implementation tell us how a chosen adhesive will age over time, thereby ensuring longevity as well as the ability to be retreated. Seeking the advice of a conservator should be your first step in addressing any structural repair to ceramics and glass.

In addition to mending, the disguising of damage that stems from filling losses and overpainting is another common form of previous restoration. Like adhesives, historical filling and painting materials tend to age poorly. While the appearance of an old fill may once have been smooth and well-matched in color, over time it can flake, crumble, and appear much darker than the original surrounding decoration. In addition, historical repairs tend to cover significant portions of original material. In removing old restorations on ceramics in particular, we often find entire surfaces spray-painted to cover up tiny areas of abrasion or loss.

While it is often the case that restorations are obvious and unsightly, they can sometimes be extremely difficult to recognize at first glance. Painting can cover entire portions of an object and be so skillfully done that it is difficult to realize that we are looking at paint and not glazes or enamels (FIG. 5). Some restorations actually involve sculpting missing pieces out of clay and glaze and then re-firing the object with the new piece; determining new from original in such cases can be even more difficult. To identify previous restorations, conservators look closely at their objects using magnification tools such as a head loupe or stereo binocular microscope in concert with different light sources. Ultraviolet light (a black light) in particular can reveal most restoration materials (see page 60 for more information about different ways of looking at, and into, ceramics in particular).

FIG. 5 This enameled ceramic jug has the left side cleaned of its overpaint, thereby revealing heavy flaking to the enameled decoration below. The overpaint was discovered when looking at the jug under ultraviolet light, as it was otherwise not immediately noticeable with the naked eye.

HANDLING AND STORING

With breakage being a primary concern when handling ceramics and glass, it is important to do so with awareness and to practice common-sense procedures. For instance, wash your hands before picking up your objects. It is actually better to handle ceramic and glass objects with bare hands, as one is less likely to drop them. You will not damage these objects by leaving fingerprints, but you should nonetheless keep finger-prints to a minimum.

Do not lift a ceramic or glass object by its handle or lid finial. These attachment points are inherently weak areas at risk of breaking. Rather, use two hands and support the object from the base or heaviest areas. It is also a good idea to move component parts separately, such as bases and lids, and use padded tables and carts when possible.

Most ceramic and glass collections are fairly forgiving when it comes to light, heat, and relative humidity levels. This relates to the fact that these materials are generally chemically stable. That being said, one should be mindful of paying attention to the storage or display of ceramics and glass in the following situations:

Ceramics with soluble salts
> **How can you tell?** You may see white accretions, or deposits, on the surface in areas of loss.
> **How should you store it?** Until you decide to seek treatment from a conservator who may be able to desalinate your ceramic, you should store the object in a place with a stable, non-fluctuating relative humidity. The key here is to avoid cycles of alternating high and low humidity, as this can cause physical damage in the object.

Glass with glass disease

How can you tell? It may be clouded or crizzled.

How should you store it? The best action to take with unstable glass is to store it in a tightly controlled environment. The ideal parameters are moderately low levels of relative humidity, set and kept to 40 to 45 percent.

Solarized glass

How can you tell? Solarized glass typically refers to nineteenth- and twentieth-century glasses that have had manganese dioxide added to the composition to prevent iron impurities from turning colorless glass a greenish blue color. However, if this glass is exposed to ultraviolet light (sunlight) for long periods, the manganese photo-oxidizes and goes from colorless to a pale pink or violet color.

How should you store it? This photo-oxidation is not chemically damaging to the glass itself, but it is disfiguring, and the color change is irreversible. If you suspect your glass falls into this category, or it has already begun to shift in color (and if this is undesirable), relocate your display away from windows or areas where it will receive excessive sunlight.

Ceramics and glass with previous restorations

How can you tell? Visible inspection, especially with the use of an ultraviolet source, may reveal restorations.

How should you store it? While ceramics and glass themselves are mostly stable, the materials used over the course of history to repair them vary greatly in their long-term stability properties. If an adhesive is suspected to have been used to repair your ceramic or glass object, keep it out of environments that experience excessive light and heat exposure, as these could speed up degradation or soften the adhesive. If metal rivets or staples have been used to repair your object, keep humidity levels low to avoid metal corrosion.

CLEANING CERAMICS AND GLASS

Can you clean your own ceramics and glass collections? Absolutely! If you are certain that you do not have any instability, previous restoration materials, or overpaint present, then cleaning can be a fairly straight-forward treatment that can enhance the look of your object and help preserve it as well. If you do suspect prior repairs, or you have any form of flaking or unstable surface decoration, then you should not attempt cleaning yourself; instead, consult a conservator.

While similar, the recommended cleaning steps for glass differ slightly from those for ceramics. Again, these are meant for glass and ceramic objects that are complete and without adhesive instability, prior repairs, or flaking decoration.

For glass (FIGS. 6A, B):
- Fill a plastic tub or bin with water and add one drop (truly, one drop is all you need!) of a mild dish soap; fill another plastic tub or bin with water only.
- Gently submerge your glass in the soapy water bin, and using soft brushes (we recommend using an inexpensive soft make-up brush), gently brush your glass object, getting into nooks and crannies as much as possible.
- Next, submerge your glass in the water-only bin, and with a clean brush, gently brush the glass again.
- Finally, set your glass on a dry towel; to avoid water spots, you can hand-dry your glass with a microfiber cloth.

For glazed ceramics (FIG. 6C):
- Because ceramics are more porous than glass (unless they are hard-paste porcelain), you want to avoid submerging them in any water bath, as this can cause uncontrolled migration of staining material or other dirt deposits.
- Instead, use soft cotton pads or cloths to get wet with the soapy water mentioned above and gently wipe the ceramic surfaces.

FIGS. 6A–D To clean glass and ceramics: (a) wash glass with a soft brush that has its metal ferrule wrapped in blue painter's tape, to avoid scratching; (b) after rinsing, dry with a microfiber cloth; (c) clean glazed earthenware with soft cotton pads; and (d) dry-clean an unglazed ceramic with cosmet-ic sponges. Whenever in doubt of a particular cleaning method, contact a conservator.

- Next, rinse with soft cotton pads or cloths dampened in water alone.
- Finally, dry with a microfiber cloth.

For unglazed ceramics (FIG. 6D):

- Avoid the use of water altogether; instead, use dry-cleaning methods such as vacuuming while brushing with a soft make-up brush or gently pad the surface with a microporous sponge, such as a cosmetic sponge.
- If the dirt is too engrained in the surface of an unglazed ceramic, you should consult a conservator to discuss options for cleaning.

USING SCIENCE TO REVEAL
THE STRUCTURE OF CERAMICS

Sometimes our eyes need a little help to uncover an object's history and condition. It is important to understand this since the type of restoration may affect how an object is treated or maintained. Different wavelengths of light, outside of the visible range detected by our eyes, can be used to discover such information. X-radiography is a technique often used in the field of conservation to examine the structural makeup of all kinds of objects, including ceramics. The equipment is similar to that used in hospitals to detect broken bones. An X-radiograph may reveal the presence of a blind crack in a ceramic vase and help detect manufacturing clues.

Ultraviolet (UV) light induces fluorescence of some organic materials. Therefore, adhesive repairs to ceramic objects invisible in normal light often fluoresce in UV light. This eighteenth-century Norwegian soup tureen (FIG. 7A) was examined using X-radiography and UV light to reveal its treatment history. X-radiography revealed extensive cracks as well as lead staples that had been filed down during a previous treatment (FIG. 7B). Under UV light, it was discovered that discolored overpaint covered a lot of the tureen (FIG. 7C). Examination using these techniques allowed the conservator to make an informed decision about treatment. In this case, the overpaint was removed, but the stable staples remained.

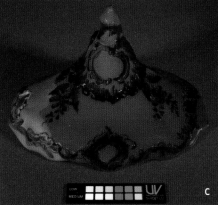

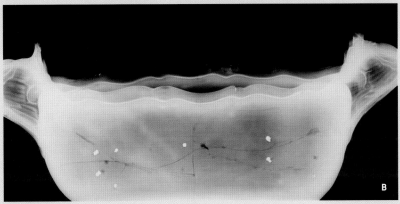

FIGS. 7A–C Upon first look, this soup tureen (a) looks nearly perfect; however, X-radiography (b) reveals that the base was broken in many pieces, with evidence of former lead-staple repairs now completely overpainted. Examination under UV light (c) shows overpaint on the lid fluorescing, another indication of hidden damage.

CHAPTER 5

Textiles

LAURA MINA

Many of the treasured possessions that connect us to our homes and families are textiles. We are surrounded by textiles that are useful, beautiful, and personally meaningful. A rug in your living room, a framed needlework piece on the wall, and a wedding dress packed away in your closet are just a few of the things that we want to enjoy as well as pass on to future generations. This chapter addresses considerations for the storage, display, and care of some of the many different types of textiles we may want to preserve.

DISPLAY OPTIONS

Many of us enjoy having beautiful and meaningful textiles displayed in our homes, whether large rugs and quilts or small pieces of embroidery and lace. Although there are many methods of display, a few common considerations apply to all. The ideal display will allow current and future generations to enjoy the textile without putting it at risk for damage.

Visible and ultraviolet (UV) light are both damaging to textiles. They can cause colors to fade and fibers to weaken, eventually leading to tears (FIG. 1). Of course, we need light to enjoy looking at textiles, but there are strategies to balance exposure with protection. Since ultraviolet is the most damaging, consider filtering out UV light at the windows or with special glass for framed objects. Avoid hanging textiles near direct, bright sunlight. Since damage is cumulative, deterioration can be slowed

FIG. 1 Light damage has caused the color of this jacket to fade and has contributed to tears in the brittle silk.

if textiles are kept in the dark for part of the year. Displayed textiles can be rotated or framed pieces can be covered with a dark cloth when a room is not in use.

SMALL TEXTILES IN FRAMES

For small textiles, it is best to frame them using archival materials. At Winterthur, we attach textiles to padded boards before framing (FIGS. 2A, B). The board is made with three layers of four-ply mat board joined with an archival adhesive. The board is then covered with polyester needle-punch felt or cotton flannel. The final layer is a "show" fabric of cotton, linen, or silk that is wrapped around the board. This fabric can either match or contrast with the collection textile. If the mount fabric shows through, a piece of muslin can be cut to the correct size and placed under the collection textile. Any fabric in contact with the

Padded textile mount cross-section

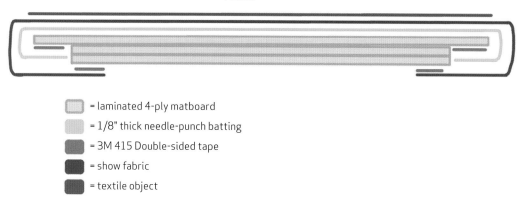

Front

☐ = laminated 4-ply matboard
▢ = 1/8" thick needle-punch batting
▆ = 3M 415 Double-sided tape
■ = show fabric
■ = textile object

FIG. 2A A cross section of the layers in a padded board used to display textiles in frames.

Textile framing system cross-section

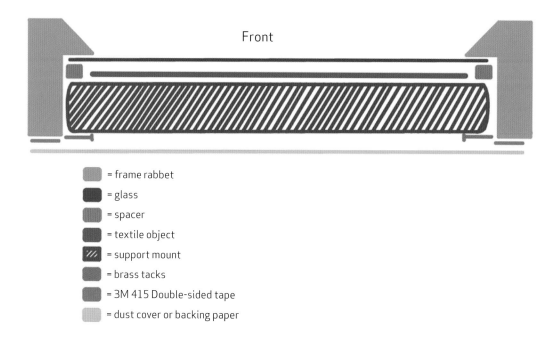

Front

▆ = frame rabbet
■ = glass
▆ = spacer
■ = textile object
▨ = support mount
▆ = brass tacks
■ = 3M 415 Double-sided tape
▢ = dust cover or backing paper

FIG. 2B This cross section includes the complete frame system.

collection textile is washed and double-rinsed before use. The textile is hand sewn to the padded board using fine thread and a curved needle. The frame should include spacers so the textile is not in contact with the glass, and the back of the frame should be sealed with a dust cover or backing paper. This system will protect the textile from dust, moisture, pests, and ultraviolet light if an ultraviolet-blocking glass is used.

LARGE TEXTILES ON WALLS

For large textiles, a band of hook-and-loop fasteners (such as Velcro) sewn across the top of the textile will evenly distribute the weight and thus prevent stress tears (FIG. 3). This method is used in many museums for the vertical display of large textiles, including tapestries, quilts, and carpets. The system is relatively straightforward but requires good skills with hand sewing. First, machine-sew the edges of the soft loop-side fastener to a length of cotton twill tape that is slightly wider than the

FIG. 3 A hook-and-loop fastener is used as a hanging system to display a quilt on a wall.

loop fastener, extending $^1/_4$ to $^1/_2$ inches on the top and bottom. If using loop tape wider than two inches, a row of machine stitching should also be placed down the center of the loop fastener. Next, hand sew the twill tape to the top of the textile with a thread that is color-matched to the front of the textile. Use a staggered running stitch to distribute the stress. The rough hook side of the fastener can be stapled to a piece of wood or directly to a wall.

FURNISHING TEXTILES IN USE

Furnishing textiles, including window hangings, upholstery, and carpets, may be better described as in-use rather than on display. Although these textiles may experience more wear, there are a few strategies to minimize the risk of damage. Curtains and window hangings are likely to experience the most light-related damage, which can be reduced by adding linings, by blocking ultraviolet light from windows, and by rotating them throughout the year. The weight of curtains can also contribute to damage; over time, tears and splits may form where fibers that are under stress break down. A hanging system that evenly distributes the weight will reduce this risk, so a sleeve for a rod is better than a series of rings. Adding weights to curtains may create an elegant drape, but it also increases the risk of damage.

Upholstery and carpets are likely to experience wear from abrasion during use. If there are activities that are likely to cause more risk, consider covering the upholstery and carpet during these times. Carpets can also be damaged if heavy furniture crushes their pile. Using carpet protectors will help distribute the weight, as will moving furniture occasionally. Of course, upholstery and carpets benefit from regular vacuuming and inspection. If dirt and soils build up, they are more likely to cause damage and attract pests.

THE SCIENCE OF DYES

The jacket in FIG. 1 is partially faded. This phenomenon is called photodegradation and is due to the breakdown of molecules that color the textile. Why does this happen? Textiles are often colored using dyes, which bond to the fiber. Dyes can come from natural sources such as roots and berries or can be man-made. The molecules making up dyes absorb certain wavelengths of visible light and reflect others, making the textiles appear colored to our eyes. Certain groups of bonds in the molecule are responsible for this phenomenon, and they can often be unstable.

The ultraviolet radiation in sunlight has enough energy to cause these unstable bonds to break or reform, which chemically alters the dye molecules, making them less strongly colored or even colorless; thus, the textile looks faded. Fading can be avoided by keeping colored textiles in low light levels.

STORAGE

For textiles that are not on display, storage systems should provide robust protection while also allowing for easy access. Although different textiles benefit from different storage supports, all need a controlled environment that is free from extremes of heat and cold as well as dry and damp. In general, if you are comfortable in a space, then it is a good space for textiles. Attics and basements are more at risk for water damage, mold and mildew, pests, and extreme temperature and humidity fluctuations. If possible, textiles should be cleaned before storage. Dirt and stains are easiest to remove when they are fresh. Stains can also weaken fibers and attract pests.

FIG. 4 As this coverlet is prepared for storage in a box, the folds are supported with padded rolls to prevent creases and tears.

BOXES

Many textiles can be folded and stored in boxes. Archival boxes are used in museums, but polyethylene plastic bins are also a good option. This type of plastic is preferred because it is more stable and won't release volatile gases. Use a large piece of muslin to line the box so that it will be easy to lift the textile without scraping against the sides or creating uneven stress.

Textiles will naturally experience stress along fold lines, so folds should be padded to avoid causing creases and tears (FIG. 4). Although there are many different materials that can be used to pad folds, Winterthur prefers polyester batting encased with medical cotton or polyester stockinette. Other possible options are polyester felt rolled and covered with muslin or just a roll of fabric. Clean, old sheets can be reused for storage support, but dyed or printed patterns should be avoided because the colors may transfer to your collection textiles. Archival tissue is also an option, but it may become flattened over time and provide less support.

FIG. 5 A hooked rug is prepared for storage on an archival tube. A piece of cotton fabric wrapped around the tube helps ensure that the rug rolls evenly around the tube.

ROLLS

Some textiles are best stored rolled, including carpets. Textiles that are long and narrow, such as lace, are also good candidates for this type of storage. Carpets with knotted pile are typically stored with the pile facing out and are rolled in the direction of the pile. It is easy to find the direction of the pile by running your hand across the carpet. The pile will feel the smoothest when rubbed in the right direction.

Museums use archival tubes for storage, but you can wrap a cardboard tube with aluminum foil to create a protective barrier. The weight and diameter of the tube should match the needs of the textile. Roll a short length of cotton fabric around the tube and then overlap your textile with this fabric (FIG. 5). The cotton header will help make it easier to roll more evenly. The rolled textile should be covered with cotton to protect it from light and dust, and cotton twill tape can be tied around the rolled textile to secure it. A tag with a picture or description of the textile can be attached to the twill tape for easy identification.

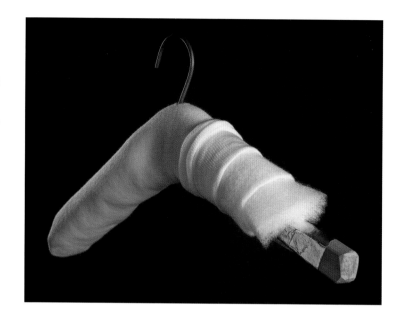

FIG. 6 The layers of a padded hanger starting with the wooden hanger include aluminum foil, polyester batting, polyester felt, medical stockinette.

HANGERS

Although many garments can be stored in boxes, some are good candidates for hanging. These include those that are in good structural condition, have 3-dimensional parts that could be crushed if stored in a box, and are not made of stretchy materials. A good hanger will distribute the weight and not create distortions to the collar, shoulders, or sleeves. Many museums use wide polyethylene hangers, but wooden hangers are another option if the wood is first wrapped with an aluminum foil barrier. The hanger can then be wrapped with polyester felt or batting to create padded shoulder support. Cover the padding with medical stockinette or cotton fabric (FIG. 6). Pants or skirts can be supported with hangers made with wide clamps. Avoid hangers with small clips; these can cause distortions and tears.

CARE AND CLEANING

In museums, we prioritize preventive, proactive care. An initial investment in the preservation of textiles can prevent irreversible damage. Within a personal collection, considerations for light exposure; temperature fluctuations; and humidity, moisture, and pest protection are critical components of care. Many textile treatments carry some element of risk and so should be done by professional conservators.

VACUUMING AND DUST REMOVAL

Textiles that are displayed without a protective cover will accumulate dust, which can easily be removed with a vacuum cleaner and soft brushes. Although strong vacuum suction and rough brushes can cause damage, there are ways to minimize these risks (FIGS. 7A, B). One option is to hold the vacuum nozzle a few inches from the textile while using a soft brush to gently sweep dust toward the nozzle. Another is to place a screen over the textile before vacuuming. The screen will limit contact between the textile and vacuum brush and ensure that the textile won't be sucked into the vacuum.

WASHING WITH WATER

Washing textiles with water and detergent can help remove some stains and soils, but it can also cause unintended damage. Dyes on textiles or embroidery threads may bleed in water and transfer to other parts of the textile. Fragile textiles may also develop tears during washing as fibers swell. Decorations like metal threads or sequins may become damaged or may transfer colors. Undyed textiles made of cotton or linen are often good candidates for wet cleaning. Others include textiles that have been washed before; those that were always intended to be washed; and those with no special finish (like a pressed moiré pattern) that could be removed.

Conservators approach wet cleaning with caution and test every component of the cleaning solution on every part of the textile. If you decide to wet-clean your textiles, these general guidelines will help limit, but not eliminate, the risks.

The supplies for wet cleaning are chosen to provide the best balance between effective cleaning and minimal risk of damage. Distilled water is preferred for washing and rinsing since tap water includes minerals that can be left behind in the textile and contribute to future damage. If distilled water is limited, save it for the final rinse. Orvus WA Paste

FIG. 7A A soft brush helps to sweep dust off a miniature bed and into the nozzle of a vacuum cleaner.

FIG. 7B A screen is placed over the embroidered seat to protect fragile threads from the vacuum brush. Cotton twill tape was stitched over the edges of the fiberglass screen to provide a smooth surface.

detergent is used by many museums for their textile collections. This product doesn't have additives such as bleaches or optical brighteners that could increase the risk of harm to fragile textiles.

Before you begin, test every fabric and thread with distilled water and then with the detergent solution. Place a drop of water on the test area and press it between white paper towels. Examine the paper towels for any dye movement. Dye transfer often occurs when the textile is first wet or while it is drying. If you notice any dye movement, keep the area pressed between clean paper towels and dry with a hair dryer on a cool setting.

A clean plastic bin can be a good container for a wash bath. The textile should be placed on a mesh sling in the bath (FIG. 8) since wet textiles are heavier and weaker and need to be supported. Cover the textile with distilled water and let it soak for a few hours. The water alone can do a lot of cleaning, and it is not always necessary to add a detergent. If detergent is used, the solution should be about 1 table-spoon of Orvus per 1 gallon of distilled water. Use a sponge to gently work the solution through the textile. Natural sea sponges or those made of undyed polyester or cellulose are best.

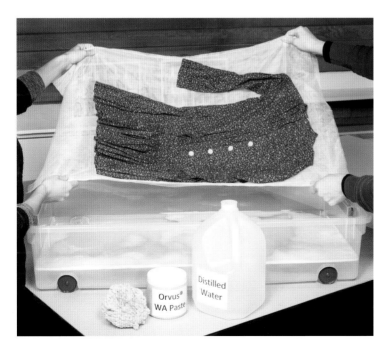

FIG. 8 This textile is supported on a mesh sling during washing.

Rinsing and drying are important steps that can significantly impact the success of a wet-cleaning treatment. Make sure to thoroughly rinse the textile, as detergent residue can contribute to future damage. Use the sling to transfer the textile to a towel; cover with another towel; and gently press out the water. Arrange the textile to air dry in a position that will provide good support without forming creases. To further reduce creases, garments can be gently padded with soft nylon net.

Of course, some stains can't be removed with water and detergent but will respond to solvents used by dry cleaners. It is worth seeking out a specialist dry cleaner who is experienced with fragile textiles and can discuss the risks and benefits as well as your goals and concerns.

FINAL CONSIDERATIONS

This chapter provides general information about methods to care for textiles. Every textile is different, however, and it is important to consider the unique qualities as well as your personal goals for its preservation. Often it is best to consult a professional conservator rather than risk causing more damage. Our memories and stories are often as important as the textiles themselves, and in museums we work to prevent disassociation—when the textile and its contextual information become separated. Photographs and written stories can be stored with textiles, or attached to the backs of frames. This way both the stories and the textiles are preserved.

FIG. 1 Photographic images from the nineteenth and twentieth centuries vary considerably. Although those shown here range in date, their processes are all based on the light sensitivity of silver halides.

CHAPTER 6

Photographs

DEBRA HESS NORRIS

Housed on phones and hard drives, in family albums, in frames, and in boxes of all sizes and qualities, photographs surround us. These treasured artifacts celebrate our lives and times and those of our ancestors; they document our world and connect cultures. Formed by the action of light on a sensitized surface, photographs made from traditional processes—such as albumen, silver gelatin, and chromogenic color—can deteriorate rapidly over time by fading, cracking, staining, and yellowing. More recent digital print or hardcopy processes popular after the 1990s, which use commercial inks and toners, may also be sensitive to abrasion, dye bleeding, delamination, and discoloration. No matter the process, many photographs are irreplaceable, and it is important that we care for them properly.

Throughout the history of photography, a dizzying array of print and negative processes have been developed involving materials such as metallic silver, platinum, pigments, organic dyes, and printing inks and toners that absorb and scatter light, thereby creating the images we see. Caretakers of photographic collections should become familiar with the photographic processes represented within their collections. Knowing when each process was commonly used, the method of manufacture, and the primary deterioration characteristics of each can help in identification and promote a better understanding of their care (FIG. 1).

PHOTOGRAPHIC AND DIGITAL PROCESSES

DAGUERREOTYPE

The daguerreotype, the earliest photographic medium to become popular in America, was prevalent from 1840 to 1860 (FIG. 2). Daguerreotypes are highly reflective, mirrorlike images where a light-sensitive silver-plated sheet of copper is exposed to light and developed over mercury vapor. The result is an image in which the whites, or highlights, are a silver-mercury-gold mix, and the dark image areas are pure silver metal. The daguerreotype plate is susceptible to degradation, resulting in corrosion films at the outer edges. To keep dust and fingerprints from damaging these fragile surfaces, American-manufactured daguerreotypes were usually sealed to a decorative brass mat and glass and then fitted into miniature cases covered with embossed leather or paper.

TINTYPE

In the tintype process, patented in 1856 and popular in America throughout the rest of the 1800s, viscous collodion was poured onto a sheet of black-lacquered iron (FIG. 3). The plate was exposed to light in a camera, dipped in developer, fixed to remove unexposed silver halides, washed, and varnished with a wide variety of natural resins. Like the daguerreotype, these images are direct positives; there is no negative. They are one of a kind. Many tintype images lack contrast, most often appearing gray with creamy white highlights. High relative humidity and moisture may result in rusting of the underlying iron sheet, which is most visible at the unvarnished edges or anywhere the lacquered surface is damaged. Tintypes were often placed into decorative paper cards, but they can be found loose, housed in Victorian photographic albums, or even incorporated into jewelry.

FIG. 2 (ABOVE) This hand-colored daguerreotype is housed in a decorative leather case. Note the highly reflective silver-plated surface and the dark silver corrosion at the outer edges of the image. Daguerreotypes were traditionally packaged with a decorative brass mat and glass to protect them from chemical damage and abrasion. The glass here has decomposed, resulting in the formation of droplets on the interior surface. Replacement by a photograph conservator should be considered. The display of daguerreotypes should be kept to a minimum, since the textile and leather components and hand coloring (if present) may fade irreversibly upon exposure to light.

FIG. 3 Tintypes were in popular in America throughout the second half of the 1800s. They could be pasted onto paper cards, housed in decorative miniature cases, or left loose for placement in albums. When exposed to high relative humidity conditions, these images will rust. Usually varnished, they may also yellow with age, as seen here.

FIG. 4 Cabinet cards were collected and treasured during the Victorian era. Those pictured here are albumen prints in various states of preservation. The one on the left has minimal fading and discoloration. In comparison, the child's portrait on the right has yellowed, with loss of highlight detail. This sort of deterioration is characteristic of the albumen process.

FIG. 5 Many of these twentieth-century black-and-white (silver-gelatin) photographs are faded and yellowed. Some are glossy and unmounted; others are matte and adhered to decorative cards. Some of the deterioration is due to improper processing, but considerable damage has been caused by exposure to high temperature and relative humidity levels as well as airborne pollutants. These prints require individual enclosures to protect them from further degradation.

ALBUMEN PRINTS

The albumen print, first introduced in 1850, dominated the photographic market globally from 1855 to 1890. Family photos from this period are likely to be albumen prints (FIG. 4). To make such a print, thin, high-quality rag papers were floated on a solution of egg white that contained a small amount of sodium chloride. The paper was made light sensitive by placing it in a silver nitrate solution. It was then put in contact with a collodion wet-plate negative and exposed to daylight until the image became visible. Following exposure, the image was toned with gold chloride and fixed with hyposulfite to remove remaining light-reactive salts. Commercial albumen prints were typically adhered to decorative cardboard mounts that varied in size, such as the carte de visite ($2^{1}/2$ by 4 inches) and the cabinet card ($4^{1}/4$ by $6^{1}/2$ inches). Albumen prints that are in excellent condition appear deep purplish brown in color with bright highlights. Unfortunately, many are faded and yellow due to the oxidation of their silver image and degradation of the egg-white protein. Their surfaces can also appear cracked because of the differential expansion between the egg-white binder and the thin paper support.

SILVER GELATIN

The year 1880 saw the introduction of the silver-gelatin photographic process, which remained popular through the 1960s (FIG. 5). In the early years, silver-gelatin prints were made by placing light-sensitive paper in contact with a negative and exposing it to sunlight, resulting in images that are typically warm brown in tone. After 1905 the sensitized paper was exposed directly to light in an enlarger, chemically developed, fixed, and washed in a darkroom. If in good condition, these prints appear black and white in color and can have a surface that is matte, glossy, or textured. They may be bright white or warm in the highlights, with or without borders, thin or heavy in sheet thickness, mounted or loose in stacks, and, if created after 1920, perhaps toned with polysulfide to create a more permanent brown or "sepia" image, especially suited for hand-coloring. Aged silver-gelatin prints are often faded and discolored because of improper fixing and washing during processing or from exposure to a poor environment and airborne pollutants. In such cases, the dark areas of the prints become highly reflective and iridescent when examined in raking light, called "silver mirroring."

COLOR PROCESSES

Color photographic materials, introduced to the commercial market in 1945, are based on the light sensitivity of silver halides and are made of organic dyes suspended in a gelatin binder layer. These images rapidly discolor and fade, creating a color shift to cyan (blue) or magenta (red) and yellowing of highlights due to irreversible changes in the chemical structures. Upon exposure to light, high humidity, or high temperature conditions, the organic dyes convert to colorless dye fragments. The permanence of these dyes varies with the process and the conditions of storage and use. Similarly, resin- or polyethylene-coated papers used for color photos, introduced in the 1960s, are prone to cracking with exposure to light.

DIGITAL PRINTS

There are many digital print processes today, and they vary in structure and stability. Three primary categories involve inkjet printers, the dye-sublimation process, and laser printers. With inkjet printers, drops of ink are emitted from a nozzle to create colored dot patterns on paper (or other printing supports). Most *inkjet-printed images* in family collections were created using aqueous inks composed of dyes or pigments on a variety of papers. Under magnification, the image particles appear circular. In the *dye-sublimation process*, the cyan, magenta, and yellow colorants are rapidly transferred and diffused to the print paper from a dye-coated, colored ribbon. This technology, most often used in photo kiosks, produces images that look like traditional color photographs. "Dye sub" prints produced prior to 1994 are uncoated and are extremely susceptible to damage. Under magnification, the images may appear blurry. *Laser printers* (introduced in 1984) are based on the technology used in photocopiers and involve dry-

and liquid-toner systems fused onto coated or uncoated papers. All laser images contain small dots; the pattern depends on the printer design and toner type. The digital processes addressed here are all complex, and their preservation challenges are significant.

WHAT YOU CAN DO

All photographic materials are vulnerable to deterioration when exposed to damaging display procedures, improper storage, careless handling, or adverse environmental conditions. High temperatures and relative humidity levels combined with dirt, dust, pollutants, and pests will rapidly accelerate deterioration. A basic understanding of these factors is critical to the long-term preservation of irreplaceable photographs.

HUMIDITY

Adverse environmental conditions, such as those in a basement or attic, are the primary cause of deterioration. When exposed to relative humidity levels above 60 percent, photographic images will irreversibly fade and yellow; binder layers will soften and mildew; and poor-quality mounts will deteriorate. On the other hand, low relative humidity levels will cause binder layers to crack or peel. Fluctuations in temperature and humidity will cause photographs to curl and distort, and their layered structure will separate.

You should store your photographic collections in room-temperature conditions with a constant relative humidity of 30 to 50 percent. Avoid humidity fluctuations of more than 5 percent. An interior closet or an air-conditioned room can be an excellent storage location. Dehumidifiers and fans may help to control the environment. Cold storage (temperatures of 40°F or lower) is the only way to preserve color photographs and inkjet papers in their original form for long periods. Low-temperature storage may be impractical, but photographs can be placed in polyethylene bags and vapor-proof containers in frost-free refrigerators or freezers. Consult a photographic conservator for specific details.

LIGHT

Exposure to ultraviolet *and* visible light is damaging to photographic materials; paper supports may become brittle, and binder layers, especially albumen, will yellow and stain. The hand-colored surfaces of daguerreotypes and tintypes (where red pigment is often added to a sitter's cheeks to make them appear "lifelike") and the dyed fabric interiors of miniature cases are susceptible to fading. Extended display, especially under bright ultraviolet-rich sunlight, will destroy color prints.

Do not hang framed photographs on exterior walls or in direct sunlight. When possible, use incandescent light (for example, spot tungsten lights) and cover windows with shades, blinds, or drapes. Ultraviolet-filtering glass will provide some protection from light, but do not place photographs directly against these protective surfaces. Mat them with acid-free materials and photo corners or lightweight paper hinges to secure the photograph into the mat. Consult an experienced framer or conservation professional for this process.

Permanent exhibition is not recommended, as the effects of light are cumulative. If you wish to display a photograph for an extended period, consider making a duplicate and storing the original. Digital prints on display are susceptible to fading of the colorants, yellowing of the papers, and embrittlement of surface coatings.

HOUSING AND STORAGE

High-quality paper or plastic enclosures will protect photographs from dirt, dust, and pollutants that can abrade images, deposit contaminants, and accelerate fading and deterioration. Such enclosures provide additional physical support and may serve as an effective buffer between the photograph and severe environmental fluctuations (FIG. 6).

The best enclosure materials consist of chemically stable plastic or paper without sulfur, acids, and peroxides. Avoid acidic paper envelopes, polyvinyl chloride (PVC) plastic (often identified by its strong odor), rubber bands, metal clips, and poor-quality adhesives such as rubber cement and pressure-sensitive tapes. Acid-free paper

FIG. 6 Photographic prints should be housed in protective enclosures and placed in boxes to protect them from dirt, dust, pollutants, and handling-related damage. Those seen here are enclosed in inert polyester film sleeves that allow the images to be viewed. The daguerreotypes and tintypes are housed flat in acid-free boxes.

storage enclosures are available in many forms and sizes. Choose those that have passed the ISO Photographic Activity Test (PAT), which determines whether there will be harmful chemical interactions between a photograph and its enclosure over its storage lifetime. Manufacturers normally provide this information.

Both buffered and unbuffered papers are safe. However, do not use buffered storage enclosures for the long-term protection of cyanotypes or contemporary color prints because their image materials may be adversely affected. The benefit of paper enclosures is that they are opaque, easy to label (use pencil and avoid ink), and affordable. Plastic enclosure materials that are suitable for protection include uncoated polyester film, polyethylene, and polypropylene. These plastics have exceptional long-term stability and can greatly minimize direct handling, since images can be seen. Both types of enclosures will also protect your images from airborne pollutants and gaseous byproducts. Oxidizing agents such as ozone, even in low concentrations, can cause catastrophic fading or yellowing of many print types as well as embrittlement of inkjet paper coatings. Acidic gases such as nitrogen dioxide can induce yellowing and bleed in some dye inkjet prints. The use of impermeable plastic enclosures will help reduce the rate of deterioration.

Matted and sleeved photographs should be housed in acid-free boxes, such as those sold by most conservation supply companies. The paper and board stock used to construct these storage boxes may be buffered. Be sure that all folders and enclosures fit the inner dimensions of the storage box so that they will stack neatly and not shift. If in enclosures and generally in good condition, photographs measuring 10 by 12 inches or smaller can be housed upright in boxes or in acid-free hanging file folders. Boxes and cabinets must not be overcrowded or so loosely filled that all support is lost. Equip vertical file drawers with upright supports of acid-free board every 6 inches.

Place miniature cased photographs, including daguerreotypes and tintypes, into small protective boxes or acid-free paper envelopes and house them flat. Keep loose tintypes in polyester sleeves or, if flaking is present, in paper enclosures. Albums may be appropriate for storing and organizing photographic collections, but look for those sold by conservation supply companies. At all times, avoid albums made of highly colored pages. Never use commercially available magnetic or "no-stick" albums since these materials will deteriorate over time. Adhesives will yellow and fail or become completely intractable.

Handle photographs with care. Resist the temptation to sort through piles of photographs, and do not touch their surfaces directly if they are unprotected. The salts in human perspiration can damage and etch the delicate surfaces and cause fading. Wear white cotton or other gloves when working with collections that are unprotected and when removing photos from paper or plastic sleeves.

WHEN TO CALL A PROFESSIONAL

Conservation treatment may be necessary for some deteriorated photographic materials. To develop a suitable preservation plan, a conservator must take into consideration the chemical composition and physical condition of the deteriorated photograph as well as the immediate and long-term risks and merits of a procedure. Further considerations are the purpose (exhibition versus storage) and scope (single item versus large group) of these treatments. Practical, reversible, and predictable conservation treatment procedures for deteriorated photographic print materials are continually being developed and refined.

Photographs that may require treatment most urgently include those that have active mold growth, flaking binder layers, degraded pressure-sensitive or rubber cement adhesives, and brittle primary and secondary supports. It is important to note that methods for the chemical restoration of faded photographs are currently unreliable. In some cases, severely faded and discolored images can be photographically or digitally copied for enhanced image resolution. Under no circumstances should attempts be made to remove corrosion from a daguerreotype's surface, as some cleaning procedures will permanently alter the chemical and physical properties. These treatments, like those for photographic prints, must be undertaken by a trained photograph conservator.

A general understanding of the nature of photographic materials will provide a solid basis for developing a practical collection preservation strategy. Many factors, including environmental conditions, storage and exhibition procedures, and handling practices must be monitored, evaluated, and controlled if we are to preserve our irreplaceable images.

ELEMENTS OF PHOTOGRAPHS

The majority of historic photographic processes can be identified visually with the naked eye or by using 30X magnification. X-ray fluorescence spectroscopy (XRF) is an instrumental technique that may be used to further differentiate photographic processes, both their final image materials (typically silver, platinum, pigments, or

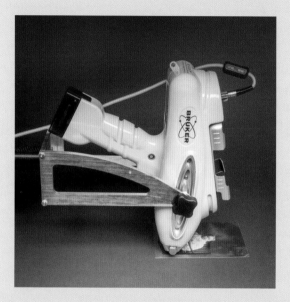

FIG. 7 A hand-held XRF spectrometer is used here to analyze a photograph.

dyes) and their associated toners (FIG. 7). XRF is a non-destructive technique (no material is removed from the object) that identifies the elements present on the surface of an object.

In photography, toning is a process that changes the color or tonality of the image and, in doing so, can improve its stability (FIG. 8). Gold toning, popular throughout the 1800s, results in a layer of metallic gold coating the silver image layer. Matte collodion prints were typically toned with metallic gold and platinum salts. Gold and platinum are less reactive with sulfur and oxidizing reagents; therefore, protecting silver images from oxidation and subsequent

FIG. 8 These images show examples of common nineteenth- and early twentieth-century silver-based photographs, including an albumen print toned with gold (left), a matte collodion photograph toned with gold and platinum (middle), and a sepia-toned silver gelatin photograph (right).

fading. Popular twentieth-century toners for black-and-white silver gelatin prints included sepia toning, which converts metallic silver to a more stable silver compound that is brown in color.

CHAPTER 7

Metals

LAUREN FAIR

Metals are ubiquitous in home collections, be they fine sculpture, decorative art objects, or items utilitarian in nature. The use of metals can be dated to the chalcolithic period (5,500 BCE), when early humans first discovered native copper and soon after, gold and silver. Today in our daily lives, we see a wide range of metals and their alloys—two or more metals or elements melted together to form a new metal—from the cars we drive and the electronics we use to the jewelry and other items we hold dear in personal collections.

METALS AND THEIR VULNERABILITIES

Of the many wonderful qualities most metals have, including strength, malleability, ductility, and the ability to take a polish or patina, they are also inherently vulnerable to several key factors that make caring for them slightly more complicated than other inorganic materials.

Physical vulnerabilities include scratching, denting, tearing, loss of plating, loss of paint or coating, and complete or partial detachment of component elements. These types of condition issues can be the result of natural use over time, improper storage and handling, or particularly aggressive prior restoration methods. When a metal object shows signs of physical deterioration, it will likely require structural conservation treatment, and a conservation professional is best suited to assist.

Chemical vulnerabilities of metals include their reaction with components in the environment such as moisture (e.g., high relative

FIG. 1 Here we see various forms of corrosion, clockwise from top left: (a) silver tarnish; (b) lead corrosion; (c) copper corrosion; (d) iron corrosion.

humidity) and pollutants (e.g., organic acid vapors). The main condition issue associated with chemical vulnerability, however, is corrosion. All metals are reactive, some more than others. Gold is considered to be a "noble" metal, which means it is the least reactive to chemicals in the environment. Iron, on the other hand, is quite reactive. In practical terms, if you were to place an iron object and a gold object inside a wet chamber for one day, the iron would corrode significantly while the gold would likely not change at all. Some common forms of corrosion on metals include (FIG. 1):

Silver tarnish: Black in color. The major component is silver sulfide, formed by silver metal reacting with atmospheric sulfur, a common component of our post-Industrial Revolution atmosphere.

Lead corrosion: Dark gray to white in color. A common form is lead acetate, formed by lead reacting with acetic acid in the environment, such as that from a wooden display cabinet.

Copper corrosion: There are many types that range in color from green to blue to red, reacting with various components of the atmosphere, including oxygen alone. "Bronze disease," for instance, refers to a particular form, copper chloride corrosion, most often found on marine archaeological artifacts or where salt water contamination is suspected.

Iron corrosion: There are many types, but colors range most commonly from red to orange to black, reacting with many components of the atmosphere, including oxygen alone.

HANDLING AND STORING METALS

All metals are vulnerable to components of our atmosphere such as moisture and pollutants. When handling collection metal objects, it is important to wear gloves. If doing so is impractical, be sure to wash your hands before picking up your precious items. Oils from our fingertips carry myriad weak organic acids that are not harmful to us on a daily basis but are to metals; they can leave their mark and etch a surface forever (FIG. 2). In our conservation laboratory, we use nitrile gloves; however, clean cotton gloves are also adequate.

One can also mitigate physical damage by following good handling procedures. Metal objects with handles, such as teapots or coffeepots, should never be picked up by their handles alone, as these are commonly weak areas that have become "work-hardened," or subject to repeated physical stresses, over time.

When thinking about how to store metal objects in collections, it is important to first consider what will be in direct contact with that object. Many materials, such as untreated wood, plastics, or even natural fibers such as wool, can emit acidic vapors, a phenomenon called "off-gassing." Contact with off-gassing materials will accelerate corrosion on metal objects, doing significant damage. When packing or storing objects, it is best to use soft materials that will not scratch surfaces and are deemed "acid-free." Examples include unbuffered tissue paper; archival Ethafoam sheeting; or even a freshly washed plain cotton sheet.

Finally, it is important to keep metal objects in as stable an environment as possible—one that is free from atmospheric pollutants and where the temperature and relative humidity are maintained within a certain range, with minimized fluctuations. At Winterthur, we aim to keep a stable temperature in the range of 60–77°F (16–25°C). In the summer months, we set the relative humidity levels at 40–65 percent,

FIG. 2 The fingerprint etched into the surface of this silver sugar bowl (see magnified detail below) was made by someone who held the object with bare hands. The only way to remove the fingerprint is to polish (abrade) it away, thereby also removing original metal from the surface.

and in the winter months, 30–55 percent; in both cases, an allowable fluctuation is considered +/- 10 percent within these ranges, based on a 24-hour time period. Generally speaking, these levels are adequate for most metal object collections. However, objects with some forms of corrosion, as is the case with many archaeological copper and iron alloys, may require a much lower relative humidity environment. For objects that are suspect, it is best to consult a conservation professional.

GOLD

Gold is one of the most stable metals although it is relatively soft and prone to scratching. Objects made of nearly pure gold require little care besides proper handling and light dusting with soft cloths or a small amount of ethyl alcohol on a cotton swab. Gold is often present as a component with other metals, such as gilding or plating, and in these cases, the gold is quite vulnerable to physical deterioration, such as abrasion. When an object is plated or gilt, we refer to the top layer (in this case, the gold) as the plating layer; the underlying layer or layers are the base metal(s). For instance, "ormolu" or "fire gilding" refers to a copper alloy plated with gold. If a base metal is corroding through the plating, which can often be quite thin, then the cleaning of such an object becomes more complicated, and a conservation professional should be consulted. Normal cleaning and polishing methods could easily remove original gold plating.

SILVER

Like gold, silver is a softer metal prone to scratching if not handled carefully. Most often, the silver we see in collections is alloyed with other metals, primarily copper. Sterling silver, for instance, is an alloy of 92.5 percent silver and 7.5 percent copper. Many objects that are sterling silver are stamped as such, which tells us that the metal is almost pure silver. This is in contrast to what we call silver plate, meaning a plating of silver over another base metal, usually a copper alloy. Like gold plating, silver plating is also typically thin and is therefore prone to abrasion and loss of material. It can be challenging to know immediately when looking at a silver object whether it is pure silver or silver plate (see page 102 for ways in which one analytical tool in particular can tell us what metal(s) we have).

Silver is extremely reactive to sulfur-containing compounds in our atmosphere. Silver sulfide tarnish is a common corrosion product; its formation happens readily and can be quite disfiguring (FIGS. 3A, B). While many commercial products are available for polishing silver, they often contain chemicals that may harm your silver and other metals in the long run. We recommend the following steps for cleaning most silver

FIGS. 3A, B We see here the "before" and "after" treatment of a silver-plated-copper (fused plate) candelabrum. Note the reduction of tarnish as well as the copper base metal showing through where the silver has worn away.

items; they have proven to be the gentlest method and offer the most control throughout the process. It should be noted, however, that some objects with non-metal parts should be treated with caution: ivory/wood handles; those with traces of original gilding or an existing coating; those with suspected original chemical treatments (an applied patina); and silver-plate objects that are known to have been electroplated (because the plated silver in these cases is extremely thin). In these cases, it is best to consult a conservation professional.

Polishing silver:
- Place the object in a large bath of water with one drop of a mild dishwashing detergent. Use a soft brush, such as a makeup brush or soft-bristle toothbrush, to gently clean the surface. Be sure to remove old polish residues imbedded in crevices.
- Rinse the object thoroughly in clean water and dry completely with clean, soft cotton rags. Do not use much pressure when drying, as even soft cloths can abrade the surface.
- Make a creamy paste by mixing precipitated calcium carbonate and water. Calcium carbonate should be purchased at a

chemical supply company to ensure uniform particle size and the absence of other filler materials. Using a soft cotton cloth or cotton flannel, gently rub the mixture over the metal surface. Only the gentlest pressure should be used, as it is possible to scratch the metal surface or remove plating if cleaning is too vigorous. As the cotton becomes dirty, change to another part of the cloth or use a fresh one.

- Once finished, wipe away dry residues and follow the cleaning and rinsing procedure outlined in the first two bullets above. It is important to be diligent in removing all polish residues, as those remaining will build up over time and hold moisture to the surface of the metal, thereby increasing the rate of tarnish in those areas.

LEAD

In the nineteenth century, sculptures cast in lead were extremely popular with American collectors, following English traditions of placing them as decorative outdoor garden elements. Winterthur's garden object collection contains numerous lead sculptures, some of which are still on view throughout the estate (FIG. 4). Generally stable as a material (except to organic acids), lead can fare well inside and outside with minimal intervention besides dusting and proper storage (if inside) and regular washing (if outside). In some geographical areas, including Delaware, however, squirrel activity can be detrimental to outdoor lead sculpture. Squirrels find lead to be an ideal chewing material and can wreak havoc on objects until entire parts are destroyed. At Winterthur, conservators routinely apply a protective wax containing cayenne pepper to their lead sculptures, and this has successfully kept the debatably cute creatures at bay.

With smaller lead objects, or when lead is a component of another object, you should consider its toxicity as a factor in handling. If not wearing gloves, be sure to wash your hands immediately after coming in contact with lead objects.

FIG. 4 This lead garden sculpture adorns the base of a bronze sundial at Winterthur. Each component of the sundial is cared for on a yearly basis by the museum conservation and preventive staff.

WHITE METALS

The term *white metal* is generally used to describe any silver-appearing metal whose alloy composition is unknown. Beyond silver and lead themselves, white metal can refer to pewter (usually an alloy of tin, lead, and small amounts of copper); the non-lead version of pewter sometimes called Britannia metal (containing tin, antimony, and other trace elements such as copper or bismuth); German silver, also known as "nickel silver" or "paktong" (an alloy of copper, nickel, and zinc); aluminum; zinc; tin; and chrome-plated metals, among others. It can be tricky to know which metal your object contains just by looking (FIG. 5) although sometimes objects are honestly stamped, telling you precisely

FIG. 5 This group of "white metal" objects highlights their similarities and differences in appearance. Clockwise, from back left: pewter flagon, pewter cream pot, Britannia metal coffeepot, pair of Britannia metal candlesticks, nickel silver fish server with elephant ivory handle, and nickel silver tobacco box.

their material composition. Even if you are reasonably sure of the class of metal, you cannot know its exact alloy composition without additional analytical tools. Makers often experimented with their alloys, using whatever raw materials were available at the time. Craftspeople use the term *pot metal* to describe the product formed by melting together in one pot the white metal scraps from various manufacturing processes. Because of the potential for much variation in alloy composition across this category, there is consequently much variation in specific needs for treatment and care. Reaching out to a conservation professional is a good place to start.

COPPER

In its pure state, copper is a relatively soft metal that can easily be deformed or scratched. As a result, it is often combined with other metals to produce a range of what we call "copper alloys." Although these mixtures can vary, a few clear distinctions can be made.

Brass is an alloy of copper and zinc, with ratios that can vary but contain anywhere from 50 to 65 percent copper. Harder and more durable than copper alone, brass still retains a good deal of malleability. It is used to produce decorative and utilitarian objects and in applications requiring low friction, such as locks, gears, bearings, and doorknobs. Brass can be polished to a high shine that lends itself to being decorative, either on its own or as a component of a larger object. It is the zinc in this alloy that is more vulnerable than the copper, but all copper and copper alloys will oxidize by reacting with oxygen alone. The zinc is most susceptible to exposure to acids and can undergo what is called "dezincification." In this process, the zinc is selectively removed along with copper oxides on the surface. In general, stay away from commercial household cleaners or remedies on precious brass collection objects. You may, however, polish your brass using the methods described for polishing silver; if more is needed, contact a conservation professional.

Bronze is an alloy of copper and tin, with tin comprising ~10 to 12 percent of the mix. Historical compositions, however, can vary greatly. Modern bronzes cast in foundries today vary further and include non-metal components such as arsenic, phosphorous, or silicon. Bronze makes for an ideal casting metal, as it can create highly detailed and nearly perfect forms. It is also a relatively harder metal and can therefore be found in monumental sizes, such as in architectural elements and outdoor sculpture. In addition, bronze tends to be more physically and chemically stable and may not need more than routine dusting and proper handling and storage. Especially in an outdoor context, bronze can be patinated by chemically altering the surface to provide predetermined coloration. This "patina" may offer additional stability to the bronze substrate, but it can be more prone to alteration by the environment or by cleaning. If an original patina is suspected on your bronze object, bring in a conservation professional to consult or carry out treatment.

IRON

Iron is one of the most reactive metals. It is sensitive to elevated levels of moisture in the air and reacts poorly with chlorides, such as with exposure to salt water. Subsequently, the corrosion that forms can be comparatively large in size and quite disfiguring. Although iron will readily rust in most environments, it is ubiquitous in collections of any type and time period. One reason is that iron is one of the most abundant elements in the earth's crust and can be worked and re-worked, cast or wrought. If done properly or alloyed with the right amount of carbon (to make steel), it can produce one of the hardest materials, useful in countless utilitarian and structural applications.

Because of its vulnerabilities, the most important tip in caring for iron is to provide a clean, dry environment for storage or display. Beyond simple dusting to remove loose surface dirt, exercise caution when attempting to clean iron or remove corrosion. Iron objects are often plated with a layer of tin, known as "tinned iron" or "tinplate" (FIG. 6). They are also often painted, and both plating and painting can be obscured by corrosion layers, thereby putting them at risk of removal if not carefully cleaned. Furthermore, because the corrosion that forms on iron tends to "grow" out of the surface, wholesale removal can significantly reduce the original size of an object and change the original shape or surface decoration in irreversible ways. A conservation professional can discuss cleaning options with you and consider appropriate surface treatments that may help protect the iron from future corrosion, especially if in an outdoor context.

FIG. 6 These tinplate and painted tinned iron objects in the Winterthur collection show signs of distress. On the painted examples, flaking is visible, revealing the shiny tin below. The unpainted example in the center would have been much shinier when originally made; however, much of the tin has been lost due to iron corroding through the surface.

A NOTE ON COATING METAL

It sometimes makes good sense to have a coating applied to your metal object, particularly if the one applied at the time of manufacture is now degraded. A conservation professional is *always* the best person to make this call. Conservators are best equipped with the knowledge and skill to choose the class of coatings appropriate for the object and circumstance and to apply the coating itself, if this is the path to take.

USING SCIENCE TO IDENTIFY METALS

Conservation scientists use X-ray fluorescence spectroscopy (XRF) to identify elements present in metal objects. XRF is a non-destructive technique whereby an X-ray beam is focused on the surface of an object, causing the elements in the surface to produce characteristic fluorescent X-rays (FIG. 7). The technique can help determine the metal in the object, which in turn allows us to make decisions about its care.

FIG. 7 XRF is being used to identify the elements present in this silver beaker in the Winterthur collection. In this case, the scientific data supported the connoisseurship evidence that the beaker was fabricated pre-1850.

When it comes to silver, XRF can also help date an object. For example, traces of lead and gold are routinely found in silver that was refined before the mid-1800s; thus, their presence or absence is an indicator of relative age. Modern refining techniques have made it possible to eliminate these "contaminants," so the absence of lead and gold in a silver object is strong evidence that the silver was refined and the object was fabricated after about 1850.

CHAPTER 8

Works of Art on Paper

JOAN IRVING

Paper is a miracle, and it is everywhere—in ancient tombs in China, in the packaging of our personal mobile devices, and in the staggering varieties of digital prints available today. Even with rapid changes in technology and electronic media, paper endures as a primary support for works of art such as prints, drawings, pastels, watercolors, and mixed media. Delicate and porous, it is supremely sensitive to the artist's pen, pencil, brush, and printing plate. Despite its seeming fragility, paper survives in museum collections and on the walls of our homes. What can we do to preserve and care for our collections at home? With an understanding of the unique qualities of paper, its manufacture, its strengths, and its vulnerabilities, there is much that can be accomplished.

THE NATURE OF PAPER

The miraculous nature of paper has much to do with its two major ingredients: cellulose, the most abundant organic polymer in the world, and water. These two substances have a tremendous chemical affinity for each other, promoting the strong fiber bonds that allow for the formation of a sheet of paper. Early European and North American handmade papers consist solely of paper fibers suspended in water and laid down on a wire screen by the "vat man," a highly trained craftsman tending a vat of pulp. These early papers were made from rags, generally linen, collected and carefully sorted by quality. The rags were chemically decomposed by being soaked in lime and physically "beaten to a pulp" by wooden hammers or, later, mechanized metal beaters. Seen today, some of these early rag papers, such as the ones dating from the thirteenth-century mills of Fabriano, Italy, are in remarkably good condition—still strong, flexible, and relatively bright.

Why are papers from centuries ago in such good condition while our paperbacks only decades' old are now brown and sometimes crumbling? One major reason is manufacture. Papers made from rags have long paper fibers, which create strong bonds and strong sheets. They were also processed with lime, a source of calcium, which is good for our bones and for paper. These early papers were sometimes given a coating of gelatin sizing to provide strength and waterproofing, allowing them to be written upon with fluid inks or other aqueous media. While some good-quality artists' papers are still made from rags with gelatin sizing, many commercially produced papers today have no such advantages. Mechanization of the nineteenth century brought many changes to paper, including papermaking machines and new types of sizing that could be implemented on an industrial scale. Alum-rosin sizing, which came into general use after about 1830, was successful as a sizing agent for the machine age but also introduced acid to the paper. Acids are known to contribute to the hydrolysis of cellulose, shortening the cellulose polymer and resulting in weak and brittle sheets. Other sources of acids include bleach and acidic sulfite processing, or the breaking down of the pulp with acids rather than lime.

The last quarter of the nineteenth century saw one other major development—the introduction of wood pulp to papermaking. Wood fibers, while also made of cellulose, are shorter than the earlier rag fibers, yielding weaker sheets. Wood fibers, if not chemically purified, contain lignin, which also contributes significantly to the discoloration and yellowing of paper. Although the "era of acidic papermaking," has left troves of crumbling paper in its wake, all is not lost. There are steps we can take to protect works on paper and to slow the effects of time, environment, and inherent vice from manufacture.

LIGHT

We need light to see and enjoy works on paper, but light can be harmful, causing permanent and irreversible damage to cellulose and design materials (FIG. 1). The types of light that are most injurious to paper are ultraviolet, visible, and infrared radiation. Ultraviolet light, which we cannot see, causes photo-chemically induced oxidation of cellulose,

FIG. 1 Light damage has caused darkening of the paper support and irreversible fading of the watercolor.

which shortens the cellulose polymer. The result is weak and brittle paper. It can also cause fading of some pigments and darkening of papers, particularly those with lignin or ground wood, such as that in newsprint. Visible light, which we can see, is also damaging to paper. It can cause temporary bleaching of some papers and fading of many sensitive, organic colorants. These colorants might commonly be found in watercolors, colored felt-tip markers, colored printing inks, and vegetable dyes, affecting not only designs but colored papers as well. The third type of light is infrared radiation, which is heat and is also problematic for cellulose.

Knowledgeable picture framers today offer many types of ultraviolet-filtering glazing (acrylic and glass), which provides good protection for paper but can also produce a false sense of security. Ultraviolet-filtering glazing only protects from ultraviolet light, one particular segment of the electromagnetic spectrum. Visible light is still problematic. If you plan to display watercolors, designs with colored media, or colored papers, consider placing them away from windows; instead, hang them in areas with dim lighting. Rotating sensitive colored materials, by taking them off display for periods of time, may also slow the effects of light exposure; it cannot, however, reverse it. For items such as diplomas, documents, or paper ephemera, consider making good-quality facsimiles for display and storing the originals in the dark for long-term preservation. The inconvenient reality is that works on paper are not suited for permanent display.

HEAT AND HUMIDITY

Paper collections are generally best preserved in environments that are also comfortable for humans, not in hot attics or humid basements. Paper fares best in temperatures between 68°F and 70°F, with a relative humidity between 40 and 50 percent. With a warming planet and concerns for sustainability, the conservation profession has moved away from strict prescriptive parameters for temperature and humidity, especially within institutional environments, allowing instead for some controlled daily and seasonal shifts. The fact remains, however, that organic materials such as paper are vulnerable to fluctuations in heat and humidity. Heat may produce thermally induced darkening of cellulose. It can also increase the rate of chemical reactions known to deteriorate paper—namely, oxidation, or the slow burning of cellulose by exposure to oxygen. Some papers are more vulnerable to heat and oxidation, particularly wood-pulp papers, acidic papers, and those with alum-rosin sizing, but all papers benefit from a cooler environment.

Ironically, one of paper's main ingredients, water, is also an enemy. It is the intrinsic chemical affinity of cellulose and water that allows a sheet of paper to readily absorb and retain moisture, which, in excess, can cause chemical degradation, mold growth, stains, and mechanical deformations of the sheet. While oxidation is fueled by heat and oxygen, hydrolysis, the other chemical reaction that is damaging to cellulose, is accelerated by humidity. Humidity, particularly above 70 percent, can also promote mold or fungal growth. Cellulose itself, a polymer of glucose, is a nutrient for fungi, as are starch and gelatin sizing materials. Even the plant gum binders found in pastels and watercolors facilitate the growth of mold spores. Mold can cause permanent staining, loss of design materials, and weakening of a sheet of paper. Fungal activity is also linked to a particular type of staining that is common to cellulosic materials, known as "foxing" due to its reddish color (FIG. 2). Foxing spots are associated with high relative humidity, with the presence of fungal spores, and with papers that have metallic impurities from manufacture such as iron and copper.

Other than mold, humidity can cause planar deformations of papers, resulting in cockling (multiple ripples as seen in cockle shells) and

FIG. 2 Reddish-brown spots, called foxing, are associated with mold growth, metallic specks, and high relative humidity.

FIG. 3 Large fluctuations in relative humidity can result in these severe distortions, called cockling.

warping (FIG. 3). These damages, however, are not just aesthetic. Rapid fluctuations in temperature and humidity can cause mechanical stresses to cellulose, breaking bonds and making cellulose more vulnerable to oxidation and hydrolysis. Humidity is a danger to not only paper but also some media as well, such as iron gall inks and the pigment verdigris. Lastly, direct exposure to liquid water, from a leak or flood, causes brown staining called a tideline, since the stain follows the contours of the wet and dry boundary of the paper. Severe tidelines are not only unsightly but also chemically detrimental to the health of paper since water-soluble degradation products are concentrated in the stain, where they can cause further chemical damage.

WHAT YOU CAN DO

Most of the adverse condition issues discussed above, including stains, tears, and planar deformations, require the services of a professional paper conservator. Nonetheless, there is much we can do to care for our paper collections at home. As early as 1844, collectors were being cautioned against handling prints unnecessarily. This still holds true today. In fact, much of what befalls a print, drawing, watercolor, or other work of art on paper is a result of our own well-intentioned actions with regard to their display and preservation.

We should handle works of art on paper sparingly, placing them on a secondary support such as mat board or a clean heavyweight sheet of paper. Paper conservators know that fingerprints, initially invisible, become visible over time as the natural oils from skin attract dust and grime. Always wash your hands before touching artwork. Keep your paper collections in temperate zones within the home. To avoid heat, do not hang framed objects above radiators and fireplaces. Rather than fixate on a particular number for the ideal temperature and humidity, aim for a stable environment. Enclosures such as folders, boxes, mats, and frames can buffer environmental fluctuations and serve as effective, sustainable, passive climate controls.

REMEDIES AND RISKS

Many do-it-yourself conservation remedies sold online and in art supply stores—ranging from sprays to "archival" tapes—should be approached with great caution. There are numerous spray and mist products designed to combat acids in paper; these, however, can have unintended side effects by diminishing and interacting with design materials. These products contain organic solvents that can cause some colored inks and dyes to bleed or shift in tone. Other spray products, sold in a variety of matte and gloss finishes, contain ultraviolet light inhibitors designed to protect against fading and discoloration from light. These, too, contain solvents that can negatively impact some design materials.

FIG. 4 In the upper left corner we can see staining from pressure-sensitive tape.

Of course, paper is porous, and whatever is sprayed on is likely to remain permanently within the sheet. One of the basic tenets of professional conservation today is that treatments should be reversible, and the chemical additives in sprays are not easily removed.

Tapes and adhesives are another source of discoloration and damage to paper. The garden variety tapes found in the office supply stores are meant for utilitarian purposes and not for the repair of works of art on paper. Sticky pressure-sensitive tapes, either acrylic or rubber-based, can penetrate the paper fibers and are very difficult to remove. Long-term, rubber-based tapes can cause significant brown stains and deterioration of the paper support, problems that can only be reduced with extensive conservation treatment (FIG. 4). Even some "archival" varieties of adhesives can penetrate the paper support, leaving the paper slightly transparent upon aging. Other varieties of tapes have water-soluble, gummed adhesives on thin paper or on linen. These pre-coated tapes must be moistened in order to reactivate the adhesives before using. This wetting may cause stains, alter water-sensitive design materials, or cause planar distortions to the sheet. In general, all commercially available tapes should be avoided.

MATTING & FRAMING

Much of what comes to the paper conservator for repair is a result of problematic matting and framing: staining due to acidic mats, stains or mechanical damages from adhesives, and discoloration from wood backing boards (FIGS. 5A, B). What constitutes a good mat? The best-quality mat boards are 100 percent rag board, made from cotton fibers,

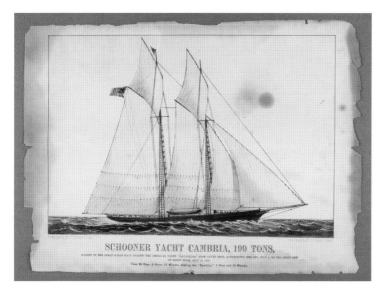

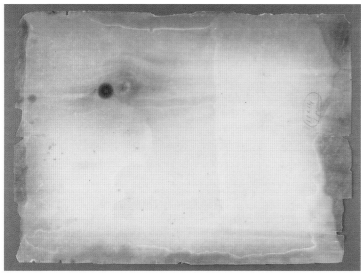

FIGS. 5A, B Paper is porous, and it will absorb volatile compounds from adjacent materials. An acidic, wood backing board has caused transfer staining that resembles the wood grain.

or 100 percent alpha-cellulose, made from chemically purified wood pulp. The assurance of "100 percent" is important because sometimes good-quality papers are used as facing papers, with the interior portion of the board laminate being unpurified wood pulp. Such boards can cause "mat burn," a type of brown staining around the perimeter of the mat window (FIG. 6). While the term *acid free* is commonly used, wise consumers should look for wording such as 100 percent rag board, lignin-free, and buffered, which means the board has a small amount of an alkaline material such as calcium carbonate. Some mat boards have the added benefit of zeolites, which are small molecular sieves embedded in the boards that absorb atmospheric pollutants and degradation products

FIG. 6 "Mat burn" is a linear brown stain in the margins of the artwork caused by an acidic window mat.

from the paper itself. Buffered boards are good for the vast majority of works on paper. Nonbuffered boards, or boards that are not alkaline, are sometimes recommended for works with sensitive dyes and colorants, such as cyanotypes and some East Asian dyed or colored materials.

The primary function of a mat is to prevent the paper from touching the frame and glazing. Most mats consist of two pieces: a front mat, sometimes called the window, and a back mat. There are many styles of mats, but the two most common are the regular window mat and the float window mat. The regular window mat (sometimes called an "over mat") covers the edges of the sheet and offers the best physical security for a work on paper. A float window mat (FIG. 7) is generally recommended

FIG. 7 A "float" window mat reveals the edges of the mounted paper object, but it offers less protection than a regular "over mat."

for designs that go right to the edge of the sheet, since a float mat allows the edges of the object to be seen. For oversize objects and for modern works on paper, a window mat is often impractical or aesthetically undesirable. In such cases, spacers of rag board or acrylic must be used to prevent the glazing from touching the surface of the paper.

The method of attaching a work on paper to its mat is just as important as the quality of the board. Some very small works on paper can be attached with non-adhesive corners, often called photo corners, but most works will require hinging for stability. Hinges are small, flexible tabs of paper adhered to the top back edge of the paper and to the back mat. Hinging should be done by a trained professional; all commercial gummed and pressure-sensitive tapes must be avoided. Hinges should be made from pure mulberry fiber papers, which are lightweight, strong, and chemically stable. The adhesive should be cooked wheat-starch paste or methylcellulose. The frame should have enough depth to accommodate the matted object, a backing board such as alkaline corrugated board, and glazing. There are many glazing options today, including traditional single-weight "picture" glass, ultraviolet-filtering glass laminates, and ultraviolet-filtering acrylic. These are all suitable for most works on paper, remembering the caveat that ultraviolet filtering does not protect from visible light. For pastels and other works with fragile media, non-static glazing is recommended, either glass or acrylic with a non-static coating. The delicate surfaces of pastel and charcoal are best protected by traditional matting and framing (FIG. 8), but some works on paper can be stored unframed. Most prints, watercolors, and drawings with stable media can be placed in alkaline, lignin-free paper folders. These can be stored flat in alkaline corrugated boxes or sturdy Solander boxes. Individual folders are best; however, if multiple objects are stored in one folder, a sheet of smooth, acid-free interleaving paper should be placed between each.

With good-quality storage materials, which includes matting and framing, paper objects are better equipped to withstand the vicissitudes of handling and display. For exhibition, the single most important task is selecting a knowledgeable and ethical framer. The chemical stability of the mats, backing materials, and adhesives have significant impact on

the longevity of a work on paper. Of course, additional preventive care includes minimizing exposure to visible and ultraviolet light. With these measures, the collector can enjoy artworks while preserving them for future generations.

For condition problems that cannot be addressed with preventive care, such as tape stains, foxing, and tears, conservation treatment by a professional paper conservator may be necessary. The national professional association for conservators, the American Institute for Conservation of Historic and Artistic Works (AIC), provides advice as well as an online directory of conservators, by specialty as well as geographic location.

THE SCIENCE OF PAPER AND VERDIGRIS

The pigment known as verdigris has been used to create shades of green in drawings and illustrations since antiquity (FIG. 9). It is a green salt comprising copper and acetate ions. Traditionally it was prepared by exposing copper metal to vinegar. It can take different chemical forms with varying pH and hydration.

FIG. 9 Verdigris degradation has caused some leaves of this fraktur design to turn from green to brown.

Sometimes called the "burning green," verdigris can discolor to brown and cause staining of the paper and even adjacent colors. Verdigris is commonly found in early maps, hand-colored prints, and German-American illuminated manuscripts known as fraktur. It can often be visually identified by observing the back of an object, where dark brown staining mirrors the verdigris design on the front. Deterioration of verdigris can be slowed by good preventive care, such as placing the artwork in alkaline enclosures and maintaining low relative humidity.

CHAPTER 9

Paintings

MATTHEW CUSHMAN

Paintings can take many different forms and serve varying functions. They may be purely decorative in nature, such as in a fine art easel painting, or the painted surface may serve a protective purpose, as is the case with architectural paint. Paintings may be as small as a postcard or as large as a mural, and they may be more or less removed from their original aesthetic intent and context.

Because traditional easel paintings appear to be simple, flat surfaces surrounded by three-dimensional frames, it can be easy to forget that paintings are complex, layered structures composed of many different types of materials, all of which impart varying physical, chemical, and optical properties to the object. Supports can range from wood panels to canvas or other fabrics, compressed fiberboards, plaster walls, and even paper and metal sheets. Artists' paints may be bound in oil, egg tempera, acrylic, animal glue, or wax. When considering modern and contemporary paintings, the materials can be even more numerous. The artist's choice of materials and technical proficiency in constructing the painting are both key factors in determining the artwork's long-term stability.

PAINTING CONSTRUCTION

Although paintings may contain any of the materials listed above, this chapter will focus on easel painting structures most often found in collections: paintings on fabric supports and paintings on panel supports. The most common fabric supports are woven linen or cotton, almost always stretched upon a wooden framework. If this wooden auxiliary support is expandable with a wooden key driven into the corner joints, it is called a *stretcher*; if the corners are fixed, the framework is called a *strainer*. Fabric supports are usually attached to their auxiliary supports with tacks or staples.

Woods used for traditional panel supports include oak, poplar, walnut, and mahogany. Additionally, composite fiberboard supports and engineered laminate boards may be found in art supply stores today. Panel construction varies according to regional practice and the size of the painting; some panels are a single piece of wood, whereas others are composed of several joined pieces.

Fabric supports and panel supports typically are coated with a sizing layer of animal glue, starch, or acrylic emulsion. The purpose of this layer is to limit and homogenize the absorbency of the support and serve as an intermediate layer, ensuring good adhesion between the support and other preparatory layers.

The application of a ground layer, meant to provide a semi-absorbent layer that imparts luminosity and tonality to the painting, is often found between the sizing and the paint film. In traditional panel paintings, the ground is made from chalk or gypsum bound in animal protein glue. A typical ground for paintings on fabric supports is pigments and fillers in a drying oil binder. Since the 1950s, pigments bound in acrylic emulsions have been used as a ground material on both solid and fabric supports.

Once the ground is applied, the artist may smooth or modify the surface texture, and a sketch or underdrawing in ink, charcoal, or graphite pencil may be executed to guide the application of paint. Paint is made from pigments or other colorants—both natural and synthetic—bound in a film-forming material that surrounds and disperses the pigment particles. The most common paint binders found in collections are drying oils, acrylic emulsions, and egg tempera. Both oil paints and acrylic paints can be applied using a variety of techniques: as thick impasto or as thin glazes; blended directly on the surface in wet-in-wet applications or as discrete, opaque brushstrokes; or built up in transparent layers, allowing an underdrawing or underpainting to show through indirectly. Traditional egg tempera technique is much more restrictive, limiting the artist to thin washes of transparent color or short, hatched lines of paint to create opaque films. While collectors may be aware of intentional "mixed media" artworks, it is important to note that paint formulations in traditional paintings may include resins, waxes, driers, and other additives that can present challenges for preservation and conservation treatment.

Lastly, a painting may be coated with a layer of varnish or left intentionally unvarnished. Although varnish offers some small amount of physical protection, its primary function is to provide color saturation and surface gloss. Figure 1 displays a reconstruction showing the layered constuction of a typical 18th-century oil painting on canvas. Traditionally, easel paintings were varnished with tree resins dissolved in solvents; although such materials remain available, synthetic resin varnishes are commonly used today. If the artist chose to leave a painting in an unvarnished state, it is important that it remain so, as varnishing an unvarnished paint film could cause unexpected tonal shifts that irreversibly alter the aesthetic balance of the work.

ENVIRONMENTAL CONCERNS FOR PAINTINGS

The complex, layered structure of a painting makes it vulnerable to deterioration from changes in environmental conditions. Each of the materials in a painting will swell and contract to differing degrees and at differing rates with changes in relative humidity and temperature, resulting in cracking within layers and delamination between layers (FIG. 2). Repeated fluctuations eventually will lead to cupping, flaking, and loss of paint. As relative humidity increases, painting materials tend to swell—panels warp and bow, fabric loosens and slumps, and sizing and paint media become increasingly flexible. At very high relative humidity, in addition to the increased likelihood of mold growth, fabric supports begin to shrink as swollen threads tighten around one another. Although fabric supports can shrink, the paint film cannot, resulting in tenting, flaking, and loss of paint. For these reasons, it is important to maintain as stable an environment as possible; avoid large fluctuations in relative humidity

FIG. 1 Reconstruction of a typical 18th-century oil painting on canvas, beginning with sized canvas at lower left, and proceeding through preparatory layers, underpainting, modeling, highlights, and varnish application at upper right.

FIG. 2 Detail of William Williams, *Portrait of David Hall*, 1766, oil on canvas, showing a craquelure pattern resulting from the artist's construction of the painting and exposure to fluctuations in environmental conditions over centuries.

and temperature, especially over short periods of time. Slow, gradual fluctuations (while avoiding extremely low or high relative humidity and temperature) are considerably less damaging to most painting structures.

Light exposure is another concern for the long-term preservation of paintings. Some pigments and colorants will fade after significant exposure to ultraviolet radiation. As such, it is best to display paintings away from direct sunlight and to choose light sources that produce little to no ultraviolet light. Some light sources, such as incandescent bulbs, generate considerable heat; it is important to keep these light sources as far away as possible from the paint surface in order to prevent cracking and desiccation. Lamps attached to picture frames should be avoided.

WHAT YOU CAN DO

Paintings should be hung away from direct sunlight, heat sources (including fireplaces), and air vents. Because those displayed on exterior walls experience the greatest fluctuations in relative humidity and temperature, whenever possible display paintings on interior walls, avoiding bathrooms or rooms where relative humidity tends to be elevated.

Paintings should be examined perhaps once a year to note changes in condition over time. If possible, keep written and photographic records. Note whether cracks have propagated across the surface or have become wider or deeper. Keep track of the location of cupped paint, raised cracks, and areas of loss. Note whether the surface has darkened with grime or the varnish has yellowed. Changes in paint adhesion are far more alarming than a dirty or yellowed surface coating; both will require a conservator's attention, but lifting and flaking paint require urgent action to prevent further loss. A strong light placed at an oblique angle to the paint surface should help to accentuate distortions and lifting paint. If a painting is flaking severely or if there are tears in the canvas support, until a conservator can be consulted, it is preferable to store the painting horizontally with nothing resting directly on the surface. Tears should not be repaired with patches, glue, or tape. If the paint film is not flaking, it should be safe to gently dust the surface two or three times a year using a soft, clean watercolor or cosmetic brush.

Check to see that the painting is properly secured in its frame. Metal mending plates screwed into the frame and shaped to hold the painting in place are preferred over nails driven through the frame and stretcher; nails restrict movement and can induce stress with changes in environmental conditions. Paintings on panel supports should not be mounted too tightly within their frames, as they require some room to expand and contract with changes in relative humidity. The frame rabbet, the recess in the interior of the frame where the painting fits, should be padded with felt tape adhered to the interior surface where the frame is in contact with the paint surface. Spacers or bumpers attached to the reverse of the frame can allow air flow and discourage mold growth.

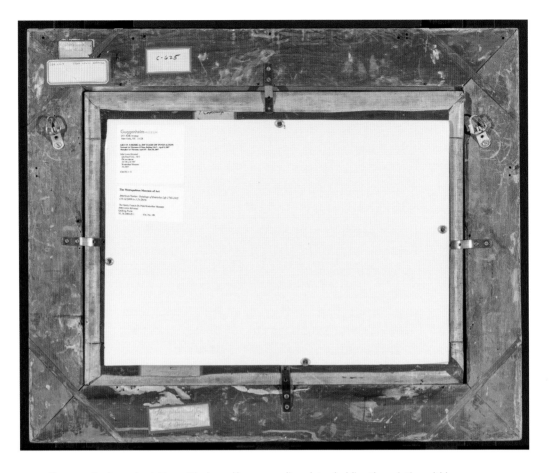

FIG. 3 Reverse of a framed painting, with shaped brass mending plates holding the painting within the frame and a protective backing board attached to the painting's stretcher.

The reverse of paintings on fabric supports can be protected by attaching an acid-free backing board to the stretcher using screws that are shorter than the thickness of the stretcher or strainer. In addition to protecting the reverse from physical damage, a backing board prevents particulate matter from collecting behind the painting and dampens vibrations (FIG. 3).

The padding of frame rabbets, proper mounting, and the attachment of backing boards are fairly easy operations; however, if collectors do not feel comfortable doing so themselves, they should not hesitate to contact a conservator.

WHEN TO CALL A PROFESSIONAL AND WHAT TO EXPECT

Carrying out successful treatment procedures to stabilize, clean, and compensate for loss requires considerable expertise. Despite the prevalence of how-to guides and flashy videos found online, cleaning a painted surface is rarely straightforward. Cleaning agents meant for household use and those sold in art supply stores often contain materials unsafe for paint surfaces, especially when wielded by amateurs or hobbyists. In these cases, some amount of damage is inevitable; often the damage is instantaneous and more extensive than can be perceived in the moment. Even materials and techniques utilized by trained conservators can result in damage if not properly applied. A small lapse in judgment or a lack of awareness can lead to irreversible loss.

Do not attempt to varnish or "oil out" a painting. Selecting a varnish coating that is reversible can be difficult or impossible without an understanding of the components of the original painting structure. The practice of "oiling out" by applying a thin layer of drying oil to the surface is an irreversible and damaging practice. Although the application of oil will make the surface appear saturated initially, over time the oil coating will darken and chemically integrate with the original oil paint film, rendering the applied coating irreversible. Applying a varnish coating of any type may make future cleaning procedures more difficult by locking surface soiling within the varnish layers.

Lastly, do not attempt to patch or mend tears, and do not attempt to re-adhere flaking paint with household glues. Doing so will make future structural stabilization more challenging, time consuming, and costly.

Contact a conservator specializing in paintings conservation whenever a painting requires stabilization or cleaning. Darkened, yellowed, torn, distorted, and flaking paintings can be stabilized and returned to an appearance as close as possible to the artist's original intent when treated properly by a professional. The most urgent issues are structural in nature. Split panels can be rejoined. Torn and distorted fabrics can be brought back into plane and mended using bridging threads and flexible but strong adhesives. Lifted paint flakes can be re-adhered or consolidated using conservation-grade adhesives, careful humidification, and small tacking irons. Similarly, detached paint flakes can be carefully manipulated and returned to their proper location.

In the case of severe damages, secondary support structures may need to be added to the original primary support. Flexible supports attached to the reverse of panel paintings will allow for expansion and contraction and accept the natural curvature of the wood panel. When a fabric support requires overall reinforcement, a lining fabric can be attached to the original fabric to take up most of the tensile forces required to stretch the painting onto its stretcher.

When a paint surface becomes so dirty that the accumulated grime results in a loss of aesthetic clarity, it may be necessary to remove that layer of grime. Similarly, varnishes may become darkened, yellowed, or dull over time, eventually requiring careful removal of the varnish coating (FIG. 4). In some cases, full removal of the coating may not be advisable due to sensitivity of the paint film; a professional conservator will be able to judge whether the process is advisable.

After cleaning, a painting may be revarnished. Typically, synthetic resin varnishes with known aging properties are chosen. The purpose of the varnish coating is the same as any earlier varnish: to provide saturation and visual depth while offering some small amount of physical protection. In a conservation treatment, however, there is an added need for reversibility as well as a physical separation between the original paint surface and the conservation materials added to compensate for prior loss.

Areas of loss can be filled with reversible putty-like materials that are textured and inpainted to match surrounding original paint or to approximate compositional elements in large areas. Conservation ethics dictate that such work be restricted to any areas of loss or damage and that the reconstructed composition be readily apparent to the viewer. Conservation treatment should be documented in both written and photographic forms, with a full report furnished to the owner. Digital and physical copies should be maintained by the conservator.

FIG. 4 Detail of an 18th-century portrait of an unknown woman. The varnish applications have yellowed and darkened over time, producing a warm tonality and reduction in contrast. Careful removal of the varnish is visible at upper right, revealing color and tonal balances closer to the artist's original intent.

PRESERVING CULTURAL HERITAGE

By becoming familiar with the physical nature of the objects in their care, by documenting changes as they occur, and by consulting with conservation professionals when treatment becomes necessary, the collector is the first line of defense in the preservation of our shared cultural heritage.

AUTHENTICATION OF PAINTINGS

Conservators and conservation scientists sometimes are asked whether they can authenticate paintings. Authentication is a complex undertaking, requiring coordinated studies from art conservators, conservation scientists, and art historians. Most conservators and conservation scientists will not authenticate paintings due to professional ethics, but they may contribute work to a larger authentication study.

Conservators can describe the materials and techniques used by the artist in the creation of the work, and they can identify passages of the painting that exhibit signs of deterioration or alteration due to prior treatment. Conservation scientists utilize analytical instrumentation to characterize or even identify components of the painting through experienced interpretation of the data. Art historians can describe how a painting fits within the practice of a region, school, or individual artist during a particular moment in time, and they can work to trace the provenance of a work of art.

Each of these types of studies supports the others in determining whether the techniques, materials, and pictorial style of a painting is consistent with what is known about a particular artist's practice. While it is rare for a single study to affirm an attribution, it is much more common for a study to be inconclusive or to raise red flags about the attribution.

CHAPTER 10

Furniture

MARK ANDERSON

Of all the fine and decorative art objects in our lives, furniture may be the most used category for many of us. We generally expect that our furniture will be pleasing to the eye and functional. In addition, we hope that it will increase in value if it is historically important or collectible. Proper care and repair will help to preserve monetary value and historic significance as well as enhance our enjoyment of the furniture itself. Wooden artifact conservation is a special type of approach that goes well beyond the limits of simple repair and maintenance. It is a more holistic approach. A multitude of publications are available that highlight specialized conservation techniques, but here we will limit the discussion to the most basic causes and remedies for deterioration of furniture and discuss best practices for its preservation.

In all conservation disciplines, we strive to use reversible techniques and materials, preserve design statements, avoid removal of original construction materials, and document or keep a record of what we do, including any initial treatment proposal. Serious collectors usually keep written and photographic records of this work in an "object file" that might also contain family information or provenance, historical research, and market-value citations from auction houses.

Treatment of furniture in use or in private collections often includes an expectation that appearance will be improved by restoring visual clarity of the surface or by making repairs and additions that are not detectable (FIG. 1). Today's marketplace and auction arenas have varying opinions about restoration techniques, and those can significantly alter sale prices or desirability. Concepts of surface patina, dry finish, original

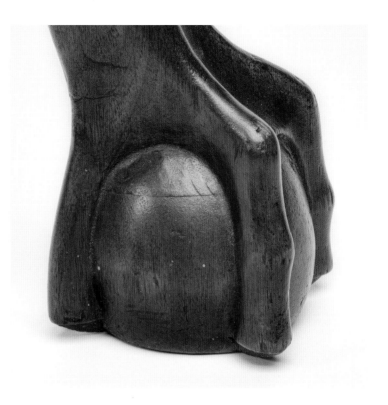

FIG. 1 This detail of the ball-and-claw foot on a Delaware Valley chair highlights a "subtractive" approach to restoration that was carried out before the chair's bequest to Winterthur. During this restoration, the feet were cut off square, 1 3/4 inches above the current bottom. The rounded ball is further disguised by skillfully placing some of the toes over the join line of the replaced ball element. This restoration sacrifices some of the existing fabric of the foot for the sake of creating a nearly invisible repair. Subtractive restorations are less common in a museum setting.

finish, and evidence of age and use all play a role in the determination of how to proceed with treatment (FIG. 2). Furniture conservation generally encompasses three broad areas: the overall structure and methods of joining; the surface embellishment and finish coating; and the added components such as hardware, mounts, or upholstery. Using a conservation approach, let's address each.

STRUCTURE AND JOINERY

Most often we think of furniture that is constructed of wood as opposed to metal or other materials. For the purposes of this chapter, we will therefore confine our discussion to wooden furniture. The appreciation of wood is ancient, dating back thousands of years. The beauty of the grain, the warmth to the touch, and the relatively light weight make wood ideal for constructing both storage and seating furniture. One aspect of wood—the tendency to change with fluctuation in atmospheric relative humidity and temperature—can create inherent flaws that arise over time, such as splits, cracks, and loose joints. Generally, wood tends to expand and contract

FIG. 2 This 1747 arcaded-drawer box has undergone several "additive" restorations at Winterthur. The left-hand drawer is newly made and replaces an out-of-period, plain-face drawer. It is noteworthy that the "line and berry inlay" mirrors the technique used on the center and right-hand drawers. The holly "line" grooves are cut with a gouge rather than compass scrapped and come to a slightly sharp termination. The front is colored and aged to match the existing drawers, but the interior parts are left bright to avoid mistaking them for the original. The drawer is stamped 2008 to further identify it as a restoration.

The finish is "as acquired" but dates to the later nineteenth century; while it is moderately crizzled, it still offers clarity and developed color that is desirable. The original feet are turned from sumac branchwood, and period dowels go through the pith into the case bottom, as the means of attachment. The lip molding on the lid and the underpinning battens are replacements. The hardware is replaced but uses a period style popular in Chester County in 1747.

across the width of a board and not along its length. Anyone living in an old house with paneled doors might notice the contraction of door or cabinet panels in the winter when the relative humidity is low. Conversely, doors and even drawer faces will sometimes bind due to expansion in summertime high humidity.

When construction techniques cross or overlap surfaces that are expanding in different directions, splitting or lifting can occur. This is often apparent in veneered furniture, where the thin, glued-on wood veneer layer cracks as the substrate below moves with changes in environment

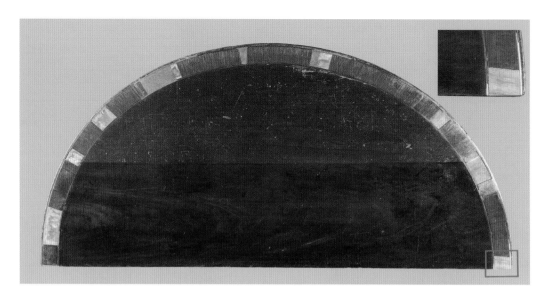

FIG. 3 This neoclassic style demilune table top has suffered damage from moisture and neglect. Veneers applied over a solid wood substrate core have expanded and contracted with dissimilar movement causing the wood to shear from the layer of animal protein adhesive. Losses of veneer and delicate wood banding is a common problem in furniture of this style. Deterioration and soiling of the once transparent surface coating is the result of poor storage or housekeeping and damage due to light and moisture. Treated areas in the image illustrate proper restoration of wood elements, surface finish, and color toning. Cleaning and paste wax yield a surface with enhanced transparency but aged coloration valued by many collectors today.

(FIG. 3). Correcting flaws due to this "inherent vice" in construction is often difficult and requires readdressing every decade or so. Heating and air-conditioning controls can help limit the natural tendency of wood to move and will help to mitigate the reoccurrence of damage.

In antique furniture, the structural connection of the individual parts, the joinery, is nearly always accomplished through interlocking dovetails or cut-and-excavated mortice-and-tenon joints. These carefully executed joints lend themselves to relatively easy disassembly and regluing. Professional conservators or repair persons will know how to reverse old adhesives contained in joints and how to disassemble furniture in ways that will not damage, mar, or dent the wood. Naturally, this is critically important to the integrity, aesthetic appeal, and value of furniture.

Let's take, for example, an antique chair that is in danger of collapsing due to loose joints. The legs and seat rails, stretchers, back support, and crest rail are typically glued using protein-based animal-hide glue. This time-honored adhesive is easy to use, nontoxic, and, most important, is dissolved by its original solvent, water. In this way, the joints

FIG. 4 The partial clamping set-up for a chair with mortice-and-tenon joints illustrates both the clamping technique and a view of the joinery to be freshly adhered with animal protein glue.

can be separated, cleaned, and reglued using the ultimately compatible adhesive, new hide glue! It's true that hide glue is not waterproof and technically not as strong as modern synthetic adhesives, but it offers nearly complete reversibility when it comes time for repair. This photo graphically illustrates the procedure for simple regluing of a basic antique chair using animal hide glue (FIG. 4).

Other adhesives such as modified polyvinyl acetate glues or epoxies have their place in furniture conservation but usually only when carefully selected and used in conjunction with new materials or barrier layers that will allow separation of the repaired area. Gap filling for rotted or missing wood is the most common use for epoxies in conservation. When making the decision to use these "irreversible materials" without a separation layer, we should do so realizing that the materials will have to be cut out to be removed. Irreversible glue can cause as much damage to furniture as loose joints or wobbling cases. Surprisingly, animal-hide glue as a separation layer with epoxy paste as the gap filler forms serviceable adhesive bonds while offering reversibility with moisture (FIG. 5). This system is also effective for cast-in-place, replacement elements (FIG. 6).

SURFACE DECORATION AND FINISH

Often the surface of furniture is enhanced with overlaid, thin wood veneers that exhibit rare grain patterns or figure. This thin layer must be adhered to a solid structural base, but the grain or makeup of the base need not be decorative. It must, however, be strong and consistent, and it may be formed from multiple pieces that are glued together. Due to the tendency of wood to move somewhat irregularly, veneers often become cracked or lifted over time, a situation that is only made worse by use and housekeeping.

Repairing losses is a challenge if a seamless blend of veneer, color, and surface coating is expected. Because wood separates along natural weaknesses in the grain pattern, working to these "break edges" makes a better repair and preserves the visual look of the original wood. Many restorers "square off" the edges of missing veneer for convenience and to save time, but matching to the natural break line is always preferable. It fully preserves original components and makes a better visual blend. A supply of old wood or discarded furniture fragments can often provide a rich source for just the right piece.

Furniture substrate woods are sometimes fully coated with non-wood materials. Asian lacquered furniture, for instance, has thick applied coatings using base-filler layers covered with a thinner film of Asian lacquer. Asian lacquer is usually a mixture of the sap from a variety of

FIG. 5 This detail shows the restored applied lip molding of the 1747 box. The edges of the box top had been reduced and re-profiled during the later nineteenth-century restorations. New replacement molding in the proper form and grain orientation were added in 2008. Note how the new capping molding form is bedded in an epoxy material with an animal-hide glue release barrier. This process is somewhat analogous to installing a crown on a tooth.

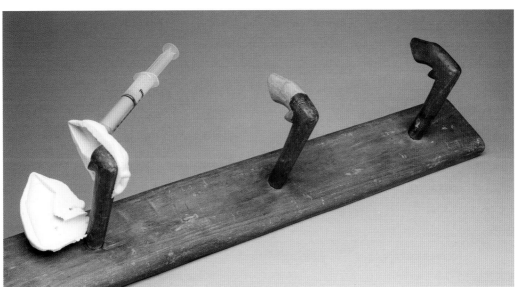

FIG. 6 A silicone rubber mold taken from a complete hoof-style cloak pin is fitted to an existing break and injected with two-part epoxy paste. Using best practices, the break edge is isolated with an animal protein glue barrier layer that will allow later separation if needed or desired. In practice, slight differences between the cast foot and the original wood element can be blended with files and chisels removing only the casting material. The epoxy add-on only can be colored with acrylic colors to match the wood; overpaint onto adjacent wood surfaces is avoided.

sumac trees or sap blended with various drying oils. In conservation, Asian lacquer, like wood veneer, is often re-adhered with animal-protein glue when it lifts or cups, but the concentration and relative strength of the glue should be carefully selected. Additionally, lacquer surfaces can develop a sensitivity to water due to light exposure, so treatment design and testing is important.

Infinishing wood (or non-wood fills) has its own set of parameters when following a conservation approach. It is best to avoid sanding or shaving down adjacent original surfaces when leveling a repair; you should work toward the patch with sharp chisels or small planes. Seal and apply color just to the patch and then apply a top coat of a suitable resin finish. Avoid "overpaint," just as paintings conservators do when filling and inpainting losses in fine art paintings.

PAINTED FURNITURE

Painted furniture, like Asian lacquer, has its own set of specialized procedures that can require the skills of the specialist conservator. Collectors of painted furniture are aware of the surface quality, muted color, and matte sheen of their pieces. Great care is *strongly* advised for any treatment or maintenance of such surfaces, and relying on the assistance of a painted-surface specialist is the best approach.

The examination of paint, lacquer, clear-finish samples in cross section and at high magnification allows a more accurate evaluation of furniture finish layers. In addition to examination under visible light, ultraviolet light illumination provides more information about the sample because different organic, and some inorganic, materials autofluoresce with distinguishing, characteristic colors. Such information is useful in understanding the manufacture of surface finishes, the presence of earlier finish applications, and condition. This sophisticated technique, which is available through professional art conservators and institutional vendors, is used by savvy collectors and auction houses to help in the authentication of surfaces.

CROSS-SECTION ANALYSIS OF FURNITURE FINISHES

Multiple layers of furniture finishes—the paint, lacquer, clear finish, and/or coating—can be evaluated by looking at them in cross-section and at high magnification. In addition to examination under visible light, ultraviolet (UV) light illumination provides more information about the sample layers because different organic, and some inorganic, materials autofluoresce with distinguishing, characteristic colors. Such information is useful to understand the manufacture of surface finishes, the presence of earlier finish campaigns, and condition.

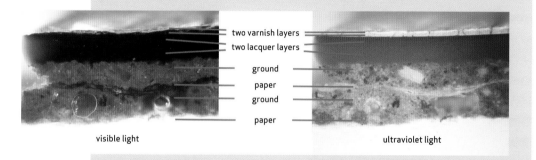

two varnish layers
two lacquer layers
ground
paper
ground
paper

visible light   ultraviolet light

Shown here are the cross section photomicrographs of a sample from a Chinese export lacquer table in the Winterthur collection under visible (*left*) and ultraviolet (*right*) light. The lowest paper layer would have been adhered directly to the wood substrate of the table, followed by a ground layer on top, a second paper layer, and a second ground application to which two distinct lacquer campaigns are applied as finish coats. Two restoration varnishes are the top-most finishes. Visual examination of the dresser table shows they have turned yellow and are undergoing severe flaking.

CLEANING FURNITURE

The buildup of grime, fingerprints, and household particulates routinely mixes with preparations for polishing furniture surfaces. Wax, oils, and sometimes solvent-based finishes combine with dirt deposits to form obscuring and unattractive layers. The most frequently asked question about furniture maintenance is "how can I clean my furniture?" The answer depends on several factors, including durability of the surface, resistance to solvents, and the overall "look" the owner wants to achieve. As we have seen in structural repairs, preserving existing materials, in this case the finish, is usually important. This plays into concepts of patina and evidence of age, which in turn can affect the value of antique furniture in the marketplace and historic appreciation in the viewer.

The first and easiest step in cleaning furniture is removing any loose dust and non-adhered dry particulates. Simple vacuuming, taking care not to scratch surfaces, can be aided by using a soft brush. Holding the vacuum wand away from surfaces reduces the possibility of vacuuming off loose and vulnerable elements. Placing a fine scrim over the brush or wand is extra insurance and offers easy retrieval if an element is dislodged.

The second step involves cosmetic or special dirt-attracting cleaning sponges. As usual, you should test first and avoid vigorous scrubbing or abrasion. It is surprising how effective these synthetic cleaning sponges can be for removing surface grime. This two-step dry-cleaning procedure is follow by wet cleaning if necessary, but the application of a quality paste wax coating may be enough to restore the desired sheen and visual saturation.

Wet-cleaning preparations should be mild and relatively neutral, not too alkaline or acidic. Conservation texts recommend non-ionic detergents or soaps as good choices, and these are usually water borne. Non-aqueous solvents also have their place if the right choice is made. With cleaning preparations or free solvent application, always test in an inconspicuous area using small amounts. "Damp but not dripping swabs or cloth" is a good rule to follow, along with gentle wiping. Don't use cheese cloth or other loosely woven fabric; they have a tendency to snag.

After wet cleaning, a simple paste wax application is the next step for most furniture (see FIGS. 2 and 3). A quality paste wax is usually a blend of beeswax and petroleum or vegetable waxes and a solvent vehicle. Sometimes a resin component is added to enhance gloss or coating thickness. Using the same cautions for dusting and wet cleaning, paste wax is gently applied in a thin layer with a soft cloth. Avoid noticeable swirls or striated build-up lines. Buff with a soft brush or cloth after several hours or overnight drying. Multiple coats of wax can be applied by repeating the procedure.

HARDWARE

In addition to woods and surface coatings, furniture often includes materials that add to form and function. Hardware mounts should be treated carefully to preserve special coatings and aspects of manufacture. Brass pulls are vulnerable to abrasive polishes, and some stamped-brass backplates are so thin that commercial polishes can corrode though the backplate itself. Any brass or metal polish that contains ammonia is particularly corrosive to the work-hardened, raised elements on the stamping. Some eighteenth-century brasses have a yellow tinted coating that changes the bright yellow color of the brass to a gold hue. Collectors value the period coating and strive to preserve it and not polish it away.

When selecting a polish, a very fine, non-ammoniated product is required. One of the least-abrasive polishes is precipitated chalk made into a polishing paste using ethyl alcohol. Preventing tarnish on both brass and the much-less-common silver hardware is achieved using a reversible metal-coating lacquer. Special nitrocellulose lacquer used for silver can function equally well for furniture brass and is a good choice.

UPHOLSTERY

Furnishings upholstery can include textile, leather, bark splint, and rush woven seats. Historic coverings can be an important piece of the history and culture of the pieces, so re-upholstery should be considered carefully. Protecting seating furniture and fixed upholstered panels from light damage is important. Abrasion and improper use is a secondary cause of deterioration. As obvious as it may seem, do not stand on upholstered furniture. For organic materials like leather, rush, and splint, strive to control the humidity; avoid dry conditions.

As we have learned, protecting and preserving furniture collections is a careful and ongoing pursuit. Counteracting the forces of nature and the forces of man requires focus, planning, and follow-through. Documenting the history of our furniture and its treatments contributes to our own appreciation of this decorative art form and leaves a record for those that follow. Common sense, environmental control, and routine maintenance will preserve and protect your heritage and investment into the future.

CHAPTER 11

Frames and Gilding

MARK ANDERSON AND MATTHEW CUSHMAN

For many of us, framed artwork turns otherwise flat blank walls into galleries of adornment and appreciation. We often take frames for granted and think they aren't nearly as valuable as the artwork they enclose, which is often true. But, as protectors of their artistic contents, frames are the first line of defense against damage and deterioration.

Sophisticated collectors, dealers, and auction houses also recognize the added value of original frames created for period artwork and the importance of backboards, inscriptions, and commercial labels affixed to nonvisible sides of the frame ensemble. As in furniture, the basic make-up of the artwork frame falls into categories of structure and surface.

Unlike furniture, the vulnerability of artwork frames is generally increased by their smaller size, our tendency to move or hang them single-handedly, and by our frequent housekeeping efforts to keep them in a fresh state of presentation. Bumped corners, cracked glass, and ripped dust covers on the backside of the frame compete with surface damage caused by caustic cleaners and snagging dust cloths. Before making specific recommendations for frame care and handling, let's address how the frame is constructed.

STRUCTURE

Frames are usually rectilinear, but oval and round frames are common. Most frames feature wood, metal or composite materials forming the rigid moldings. Typically, lengths of wood are shaped with machine or hand tools to form undulating profiles made of hollow coves, rounds, and interspersed flats combined to create the frame molding. These moldings can be further enhanced with carved or applied decoration. In most cases, a single piece of wood makes up the shaped molding but it is not uncommon for it to be built up of multiple pieces of wood glued together before shaping. The joined or laminated frame can have special vulnerabilities if exposed to damp conditions that can lead to separation along the glue lines. Plain-grained, easily shaped wood species are used, but wood species like oak with strong grain patterns do predominate during certain time periods and in specific regions where those woods are abundant.

SURFACE

In addition to carved embellishments or applied ornament, the artwork frame might have a transparent, painted, faux-grained, metal powder, or metal foil (metal leaf) surface. Some of these coatings are more durable than others. The metal leaf surfaces are particularly sensitive to abrasion, moisture, and nearly all liquid cleaners (FIG. 1). Additionally, damages due to poor handling are common, not only due to abrasion but also to the deposition of salts and greases, which come from direct contact with the skin and result in fingerprints visible in the frame surface. Because it is so easy to mar a gilded frame surface (FIG. 2), and because surface particulate is easily captured in a frame's three-dimensional profile, it is unfortunately common to see frames that have been coated with metallic paints in an attempt to regain a smooth, reflective surface. These metallic paints corrode with time, changing from a gold-colored or brassy appearance to a dull, dark greenish brown. This corroded paint is visually disfiguring and difficult to remove without damaging underlying original surface.

FIG. 1 Spray cleaners can mist alkaline detergent onto frame components. Often, the lower molding on a picture frame or mirror has much of its gold leaf or painted surface removed right down to the foundation coating or to the wood, as is the case on this waxwork diorama. Glazing and mirrors can be carefully cleaned by using a damp, but not dripping, folded soft cloth or paper towel swabs. Avoid cleaning anything but the glass. Acrylic glazing can be cleaned with microfiber cloths that will not introduce scratches into the surface. When in doubt, test a very small area in an inconspicuous location before cleaning the glazing.

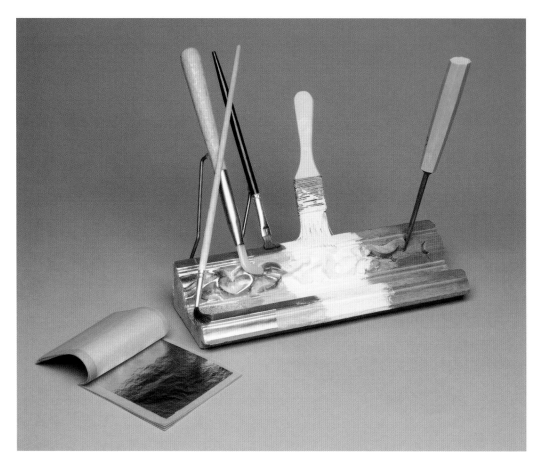

FIG. 2 The sequential layering on a carved molding illustrates the materials and process used for creating a gold leaf surface. The carved wood is sized with a wash coat of animal protein glue as a sealer and initial adhesive. The built-up coats of white "gesso" are made up of finely powdered calcium carbonate or calcium sulfate, known as "gilders whiting," suspended in an aqueous binder of animal glue. Successive layers are smoothed and mechanically leveled. A final coating of "bole," ultra-fine red mineral-clay particles bound in protein glue, is applied and smoothed as finely as possible. The fragile gold leaf is layered onto the bole surface after it is activated with a sparing, brush coat of "gilders liquor," an alcohol/glue size mixture. The reactivation of the animal protein glue, combined with changing surface tension as the thin gold leaf stretches flat, adheres the metal. Burnishing with a polished agate stone creates the brilliant look we associate with gilded wood.

GLAZING

Fine art paintings on canvas or wooden board historically did not use protective glass, while drawings, sketches, and printed works on paper did use glass "glazing." Standard glass provides a transparent barrier against abrasion, dust, and unintended splashed liquids or temporary humid conditions, but it does not do a very good job of filtering harmful ultraviolet energy present in natural light. Sometimes, artwork is in direct contact with the glass creating a microenvironment subject to mold growth and/ or moisture-induced adhesion of the artwork to the glass. Most museums and knowledgeable collectors try to rehouse their artwork within a "frame package" using spacers or mats of acid free paper board sealed around the edges. Special UV-filtering acrylic glazing can be substituted for traditional glass, and this is often the case for museum artwork sent out on loan. It can be important to retain the original glass; in some situations, it might be best to limit light exposure by taking care to place the artwork away from strong and direct light, leaving the original glass in place.

DOS AND DON'TS FOR ART FRAMES

- **Do** use care when hanging or storing frames. Interleaf frames with acid-free cardboard when storing or moving groups of frames. Avoid stacking frames, even if they are interleafed. Use hangers and picture wire with appropriate weight-bearing specifications, and always make sure the hardware attachments are tight.
- **Do** address weak or open miters joints in frames, which can lead to racking of the housed artwork or intrusion of dust and grime into the glazed artwork frame. Re-securing corners is best left to professionals.
- **Do** seek the help of experienced picture framers to create acid-free housing packages.
- **Do** use soft "mop" brushes similar to high quality soft cosmetic brushes for dust removal.
- **Don't** throw out original backing papers that have important information or inscriptions. These can be incorporated into the new housing package or stored in the object file that you keep on each object in your collection. The same is true for original backing boards.
- **Don't** use spray cleaners when attempting to clean the glass in front of framed artwork. Use a clean, damp cloth instead to avoid getting a mist on the frame.
- **Don't** subject artwork frames to strong or direct light or to abrupt changes in temperature or humidity.

THE INSTRUMENTAL ANALYSIS OF FRAME FINISHES

The finish history of gilt frames is best understood by examination of the finishes using cross-section microscopy (*see chapter 10 sidebar*) combined with the instrumental technique of scanning electron microscopy with energy dispersive spectroscopy (SEM-EDS).

Bronze overpaint
Original gilding
Bole
Glue size layer
Gesso layer

50 µm

BSE

40 µm

FIG. 3 This image is a cross-section photomicrograph of a sample from a frame under visible light (left), an electron microscope image of the cross-section (middle), and an image of the cross-section generated with elemental mapping (right), which shows the presence of copper (represented in green) from a bronze paint applied over the original gilt finish (with elemental gold represented in red).

The scanning electron microscope (SEM) allows high magnification of the sample, and the energy dispersive spectrometer (EDS) detects X-ray energies emitted from the surface of the sample to indicate its elemental composition. The instrument software produces false-color elemental maps that show where on the cross-section sample different elements are present.

SEM-EDS analysis of a frame cross-section here indicates that the frame was originally gilt with gold (Au). The frame was then repainted at a later point with bronze paint. (The term bronze paint is a misnomer; the material actually consists of a brass, i.e. copper-zinc, alloy.) The practice of repainting gilt frames with bronze paint is fairly common as the condition of gilt leaf is often compromised over time. Bronze paint is an inexpensive and easily accessible material that immediately gives a bright, warm reflective surface similar to gold. However, bronze paint is also susceptible to degradation over time resulting in black corrosion. Removal of bronze paint is usually best accomplished if the underlying gilt layer is "water gilt," which offers a dissimilar solubility factor. Removal of bronze paint over an underlying oil gilt layer is much more difficult, if not impossible.

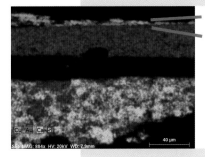

Bronze overpaint (green color)

Original gilding (red color)

Resources

Professional Organizations

**AMERICAN INSTITUTE FOR
CONSERVATION (AIC)**
727 15th Street NW, Suite 500
Washington, DC 20005
202.452.9545
www.culturalheritage.org

**AMERICAN ALLIANCE OF MUSEUMS
(AAM)**
2451 Crystal Drive, Suite 1005
Arlington, VA 22202
202.289.1818
www.aam-us.org

**INTERNATIONAL COUNCIL OF
MUSEUMS – COMMITTEE FOR
CONSERVATION (ICOM-CC)**
ICOM Maison de l'Unesco
1, rue Miollis
75732 Paris cedex 15 France
+ 39 334 730 7713
www.icom-cc.org

**INTERNATIONAL INSTITUTE FOR
CONSERVATION OF HISTORIC AND
ARTISTIC WORKS (IIC)**
3 Birdcage Walk
Westminster,
London, SW1H 9JJ UK
+44 (0)20 7799 5500
www.iiconservation.org

**CANADIAN ASSOCIATION FOR
CONSERVATION OF CULTURAL
PROPERTY (CAC)**
1554 Carling Avenue, Unit 268
Ottawa ON K1Z 7M4 Canada
613.231.3977
www.cac-accr.ca

The American Institute for Conservation (AIC) is, as stated on their website, the national membership organization supporting conservation professionals in preserving cultural heritage by establishing and upholding professional standards, promoting research and publications, providing educational opportunities, and fostering the exchange of knowledge among conservators, allied professionals, and the public.

AIC provides a free service to private individuals interested in locating a conservator. Visit https://www.culturalheritage.org/about-conservation/ find-a-conservator. An online tool will help you find the right person for your needs based on your input, such as the type of object needing treatment and your location, and then provide a list of AIC member conservators who meet the stated criteria. There is an advanced search option for specialized types of materials or types of skills/services. For more information about AIC services, visit the general website http://www.culturalheritage.org.

Suggested Readings

Adelstein, Peter Z. *IPI Media Storage Quick Reference*. Rochester, NY; Image Permanence Institute, Rochester Institute of Technology, 2004.

Appelbaum, Barbara. *Preserve, Protect and Defend: A Practical Guide to the Care of Collections*. New York: Barbara Appelbaum Books, 2018.

Bachmann, Konstanze, ed. *Conservation Concerns: A Guide for Collectors and Curators*. Washington, D.C.: Smithsonian Institution Press, 1992.

Baldwin, Gordon and Martin C. Jürgens. *Looking at Photographs: A Guide to Technical Terms, Revised edition*. Santa Monica, CA: J. Paul Getty Museum, 2009.

Boersma, Foekje. *Unravelling Textiles: A Handbook for the Preservation of Textile Collections*. London: Archetype Publications Ltd., 2007 English Translation from Dutch (2000).

Ellis, Margaret H. *The Care of Prints and Drawings*. 2nd ed. Lanham: Rowman & Littlefield, 2017.

Koob, Stephen P. *Conservation and Care of Glass Objects*. London: Archetype Publications, 2006.

Long, Jane S., and Richard W. Long. *Caring for Your Family Treasures*. New York: Harry N. Abrams, Inc., 2000.

MacLeish, Bruce A. *The Care of Antiques and Historical Collections*. Nashville: American Association for State and Local History, 1985.

Mailand, Harold F., and Dorothy Stites Alig. *Preserving Textiles: A Guide for the Nonspecialist*. Indianapolis: Indianapolis Museum of Art, 1999.

McGiffen, Robert F. Jr. *Furniture Care and Conservation*. Nashville: American Association for State and Local History, 1983.

Lavédrine, Bertrand, with Jean-Paul Gandolfo, John McElhone, and Sybille Monod. *Photographs of the Past: Process and Preservation*. Los Angeles, CA: Getty Publications, English translation 2009.

National Committee to Save America's Cultural Collections. *Caring for Your Collections*. New York: Harry N. Abrams, 1992.

National Trust. *The National Trust Manual of Housekeeping: Care and Conservation of Collections in Historic Homes*. Wiltshire, Eng.: The National Trust, 2011 revised edition.

Quye, Anita, and Colin Williamson. *Plastics: Collecting and Conserving*. Edinburgh: National Museums of Scotland, 1991.

Reilly, James M. *Care and Identification of Nineteenth-Century Photographic Prints*. Kodak Publication G-2S. Rochester, N.Y.: Eastman Kodak Co., 1986.

Rivers, Shayne. *Conservation of Furniture*. Oxford: Butterworth-Heinemann, 2003.

Shelley, Marjorie. *The Care and Handling of Art Objects*. Rev. ed. New York: Metropolitan Museum of Art, 2019.

Thomson, Garry. *The Museum Environment*. London: Butterworths, 1986.

Williams, Don, and Louisa Jaggar. *Saving Stuff: How to Care For and Preserve Your Collectibles, Heirlooms, and Other Prized Possessions*. New York: Fireside: Simon & Shuster, 2005.

Williams, Nigel; *Porcelain Repair and Restoration*. 2d ed. London: Trustees of the British Museum Press, 2002.

Websites with Collections Care Information

https://learning.culturalheritage.org/caring-treasures
Caring for Your Treasures, American Institute for Conservation

https://community.culturalheritage.org/communities/community-home?CommunityKey=efc8a209-1e74-4c1b-80d7-cb26db836184
Connecting to Collections Care (C2CC), through AIC

https://www.canada.ca/en/conservation-institute/services/conservation-preservation-publications/canadian-conservation-institute-notes.html
Canadian Conservation Institute (CCI) notes

https://ccaha.org/resources
Conservation Center for Art & Historic Artifacts Guides and Fact Sheets

http://www.graphicsatlas.org/
**Image Permanence Institute – Graphics Atlas,
Rochester Institute of Technology**

https://www.archives.gov/preservation
National Archives

https://www.nps.gov/museum/publications/conserveogram/cons_toc.html
Conserve O Gram, National Parks Service Museum Management Program

https://www.nedcc.org/free-resources/overview
Northeast Document Conservation Center

https://www.si.edu/mci/english/learn_more/taking_care/index.html
Smithsonian Museum Conservation Institute

http://www.vam.ac.uk/page/c/caring-for-your-possessions/
Victoria & Albert Museum

Selected List of Suppliers

ARCHIVAL PRODUCTS
1801 Thompson Avenue
Des Moines, IA 50316-2751
800.526.5640
888.220.2397 (fax)
www.archival.com

BENCHMARK
P.O. Box 214
Rosemont, NJ 08556
609.397.1131
609.397.1159 (fax)
www.benchmarkcatalog.com

CONSERVATION RESOURCES
7350 A Lockport Place
Lorton, VA 22079
800.634.6932
703.321.0629 (fax)
www.conservationresources.com
sales@conservationresources.com

GAYLORD ARCHIVAL
Syracuse, NY 13221-14901
800.448.6160
800.272.3412 (fax)
www.gaylord.com

HOLLINGER METAL EDGE, INC.
9401 Northeast Dr.
Fredericksburg, VA 22408
800.634.0491
800.947.8814 (fax)
www.hollingermetaledge.com

MUSEUM SERVICES
385 Bridgeport Way
South St. Paul, MN 55075
651.450.8954
www.museumservicescorporation.com
info@museumservicescorporation.com

TALAS
330 Morgan Avenue
Brooklyn, NY 11211
212.219.0770
www.talasonline.com

TESTFABRICS, INC.
P.O. Box 26
West Pittston, PA 18643
570.603.0432
507.603.0433 (fax)
www.testfabrics.com
info@testfabrics.com

UNIVERSITY PRODUCTS, INC.
ARCHIVAL DIVISION
517 Main Street
Holyoke, MA 01040
800.628.1912
800.532.9281
www.universityproducts.com
info@universityproducts.com

About the Authors

The following current and former staff members authored and contributed to *Caring for Your Cherished Objects: The Winterthur Guide:*

MARK ANDERSON, Furniture Conservator Emeritus

MATTHEW CUSHMAN, Conservator of Paintings

WILLIAM DONNELLY, Assistant Preventive Conservator

LAUREN FAIR, Conservator of Objects

JOY GARDINER, Director of Conservation

ROSIE GRAYBURN, PH.D., Associate Scientist

JOAN IRVING, Senior Conservator of Paper

LARA KAPLAN, Conservator of Objects

GREGORY LANDREY, Director of Academic Affairs

CATHERINE MATSEN, Scientist

MATTHEW MICKLETZ, Manager of Preventive Conservation

LAURA MINA, Associate Conservator of Textiles

MELISSA TEDONE, PH.D., Associate Conservator of Books and Library Materials

DEBRA HESS NORRIS is director of the Winterthur/University of Delaware Program in Art Conservation and chair and professor of photograph conservation, Department of Art Conservation, University of Delaware.

JOELLE D. J. WICKENS, PH.D., is an assistant professor of preventive conservation and the associate director of the Winterthur/University of Delaware Program in Art Conservation.